WAY OF THE ELVES

A Nine Worlds Saga

Also by Douglas "Dag" Rossman:

The Dragonseeker Saga: New Tales of the Nine Worlds
The Nine Worlds: A Dictionary of Norse Mythology
The Northern Path: Norse Myths and Legends Retold . . .
    and What They Reveal
Theft of the Sun and Other New Norse Myths
Valhalla in America: Norse Myths in Wood at Rock Island
    State Park, Wisconsin

WAY OF THE ELVES

A Nine Worlds Saga

written by
Douglas "Dag" Rossman

illustrated by
Kirsten Sevig

Skandisk, Inc., Bloomington, Minnesota

Skandisk, Inc.
6667 West Old Shakopee Road, Suite 109
Bloomington, Minnesota 55438
www.skandisk.com

Printed in the United States of America

ISBN: 978-1-57534-078-4

Library of Congress Control Number: 2012938857

Cover design and illustrations by Kirsten Sevig

Cover photo is a motif from the door of a stave church, photographed at the
Univeristy Museum of Cultural Heritage, Oslo.
Cover photo © Marieke Kuijjer, GNU Free Documentation License

Printed in the United States of America
16 15 14 13 12   1 2 3 4

The bonus story, "Trolls in the Mist," appeared previously in *Mythic Circle*
(Vol. 32, 2010) as part of a longer story, "The Walker in Shadows."

DEDICATION

To those lovers of Nature who seek to
discover—or to restore—a vision of Alfheim
in our own world and time.

Acknowledgments

First and foremost, I want to thank my three "Norns"—Sharon Rossman, Jodie Forrest, and Emily Mineart. They critically read the entire manuscript and offered detailed suggestions for improvements, not only in matters of grammar and syntax but also with regard to the presentation of the narrator's feminine perspective (Aelas, after all, is a young female . . . and I am neither).

In addition to those three women, C. Dean Andersson, Kristin Torresdal, April Snellgrove, Meph Broussard, Sally Budd, and the Alfheim book discussion group of the Mythopoeic Society have been fans of my Nine Worlds tales for many years and an ongoing source of encouragement.

I continue to have a deep appreciation for the folks at Skandisk, Inc. (Mike and Else Sevig, Kirsten Desjardins, and Lisa Hamnes) who make it possible for me to share with my readers these new stories from the Nine Worlds.

Finally, I remain deeply grateful to the people of Scandinavia whose rich mythology and folklore have inspired my own Nordic imagination and helped give form to its expression.

WAY OF THE ELVES

A NINE WORLDS SAGA

INTRODUCTION:

SPIRIT SONGS OF ALFHEIM

As some of my readers will recall, near the end of *The Dragonseeker Saga*, its protagonist, Dag Ormseeker, is exiled from his beloved Alfheim and his adopted "family" there . . . not to return for three long years. Perhaps you, like me, were left wondering what transpired in Alfheim during his absence. What, for example, did the wise elf-wizard Formindar, Dag's sworn-brother, do to pass that time? In *Way of the Elves* we are about to learn some surprising things about who Formindar really is and what mysterious powers he possesses.

As for Aelas, Dag's fang-mate, surely an elf-maid as spunky and self-reliant as she is would not spend all her waking hours moping about and pining for him. Dag's exile proves to be a time of learning and growth for her as well while she and her Uncle Formindar wander throughout Alfheim . . . and even venture into the frozen realm of the much-dreaded Frost Giants!

But amid all the exciting adventures, this book is about love in many of its manifestations—love for a particular person, for family and friends, for animals, and for the land itself. Each story can be an elvish spirit song that, interwoven with the others, creates a harmony of love. I hope you will enjoy reading these spirit songs of Alfheim.

> Douglas "Dag" Rossman
> "Ormsgard"
> Decorah, Iowa
> December 2011

P.S. For those who may wish to pronounce aloud the Elvish names in this book, a guide appears on pages 98-100.

HEART OF AN ELF-MAID

Prologue

Nowhere in the Nine Worlds is there a more mysterious realm than Alfheim, home of the legendary Light Elves. And it was to this enchanting—and enchanted—land that the Norse god Odin All-Father sent the young, half-human storyteller Dag Ormseeker to learn the lore of his elvish heritage.

As *wyrd* would have it, the first elf that Dag encountered after his arrival in Alfheim was the wizard Formindar, whose life was being threatened by a ravenous water-troll. Dag was able to save Formindar, who in turn insisted that they become sworn-brothers and share the elf's tent during Dag's stay in Alfheim.

Over the course of the ensuing year, Formindar mentored Dag in elven lore and life-ways, always emphasizing the need to acquire patience and serenity—a state the Light Elves call *lotkulas*. Eventually, Formindar asked Dag to partner with his niece, the elf-maid Aelas, in the Great Hunt, a perilous rite of passage that required seeking out and slaying a wild fen-orm in the marshes of Maras.

Dag and Aelas barely survived their ordeal, but survive they did and when they returned to their village bearing the proofs of their success, they shared in the ritual that symbolized their attaining full adulthood in the eyes of the tribe. This ritual also bound them together forever as fang-mates, of which few bonds in the Nine Worlds are closer.

An ecstatic Dag felt that he had truly found a new home, and he would have liked nothing better than to spend the rest of his life in Alfheim. Alas for Dag and his new-found family, Odin had other plans . . . .

Aelas's Tale

When Odin's raven ordered Dag to leave Alfheim at once to resume the storytelling mission Odin had given him—and then had the nerve to tell me I was forbidden to accompany my fang-mate—well, I was sorely tempted to lose my temper. That was no longer possible, however, because my feelings of anger had been sealed up in my dragon's fang amulet that Dag now wore around his neck for safekeeping. I had to remain calm in spite of myself!

The raven was having none of my protests and, when I would have persisted, my uncle, Formindar, silenced me with a slightly raised hand, the hint of a frown, and a brief shake of his head. He realized there was no arguing the will of Odin, and that getting upset with the messenger wouldn't help the situation, wasn't fair to the raven, and could well lose any possible good will the bird might have toward us.

And Uncle Formindar proved to be right . . . as he usually is. He spoke to the raven calmly and respectfully, and although I still was not permitted to accompany Dag, the bird conceded that Ledgi, Dag's newly acquired dog-companion, could do so.

So, despite my having completed successfully the rituals that mark an elf's passage into adulthood, I clearly still had a lot to learn. That revelation didn't discourage me in the least, however, because elves are so long-lived that I should surely have more than ample time to learn all manner of things . . . including the proper etiquette for dealing with annoying ravens!

The rest of that day passed all too quickly, for Dag needed to visit the other members of our village to thank them for all their kindnesses to him over the past year, and to bid them farewell. Most of them had become quite fond of him, and they were sad to see him go. But they, too, knew that there was no gainsaying the will of Odin All-Father.

As the next day dawned, my uncle declared that he and I would accompany Dag as far as the border of the Alfmark, but we would have to part from him there . . . we to return to our village, and Dag to re-enter the lands of mortal men.

"You don't need to put yourself to all that trouble, Uncle Formindar. I'm perfectly capable of seeing Dag safely on his way all by myself," I responded in a slightly miffed tone.

"Oh, I don't question your capability, my dear girl," Formindar replied. "But I also know you to be a bit impetuous at times . . . and I think you are also perfectly capable of following Dag out of Alfheim if the spirit moved you to do so. Besides," he added when he noticed me grimace slightly at having my inner thoughts read so easily, "would you deny me the chance to spend a few more days with my sworn-brother? Our bond is different than that of two fang-mates . . . but it may be just as strong."

My embarrassment at having overlooked the closeness between Dag and my uncle quickly erased any annoyance I had felt over not being able to have Dag's company all to myself . . . and not being entirely trusted to heed Odin's command.

So, bidding farewell to my mother, Falan, and my father, Skuttar, the three of us strode off toward the Alfmark, accompanied by our dogs—Dag's Ledgi and my Darra. Uncle Formindar had not yet found it in his heart to replace his dog-companion, Linu, who had been killed by a water-troll the day that Dag and Formindar first met. We walked along at a fairly brisk pace, for one never knows when Odin may be watching from his high seat—lofty Hlidskjalf—and we didn't want the All-Father to think that Dag wasn't obeying his command in a timely fashion.

The time seemed to fly by, and all too soon we found ourselves standing at the crest of the pass leading down into the Alfmark, the sometimes unruly borderland that separates Alfheim from Midgard. Although the countryside surrounding the hill-fort of Yngve Elf-Brow, King of the Alfmark, is peaceful enough, some of the outlying areas harbor outlaws who have fled from justice in Midgard. I was worried about Dag's safety once he entered the Alfmark, and I wasn't hesitant to say so!

"It is wise for a traveler to be alert at all times," my uncle replied, "but I really don't think Dag has much to fear. He doesn't have the look of a prosperous trader . . . and storytellers are welcome almost everywhere they go, even among outlaws."

"Besides," Dag chuckled, "with my iron hand and dragon staff, I'm not exactly helpless if some ruffian tries to push me around, though hopefully it won't come to that. I can usually talk my way out of most confrontations."

"That's all well and good if there are only one or two men," I said anxiously, "but what if there's a gang of them?"

"Worse come to worst," Dag assured me, "I do know how to use some very effective protection runes."

"I'm glad you recognize that to be a last resort, Dag," interjected Uncle Formindar. "The expenditure of magical power always comes at a cost . . . a cost you rarely learn until later. No, when you can, it is better to embrace *lotkulas* and avoid giving offense to those who are looking for trouble.

"Now has come the time for a parting of our ways, though—Odin willing—not for longer than loving hearts and minds can bear. Go with the blessings of your sworn-brother . . . and heed the advice the raven gave you: carry out the task that Odin assigned you, and always hope for the best. You will be ever in our thoughts until the day you walk again on Alfheim's blessed soil."

Dag and Formindar embraced, then my uncle stepped aside so I could say my farewell to my fang-mate. Now that the moment was upon us, I found it even more difficult to say goodbye than I had expected. I threw myself into Dag's arms and pressed my face against his chest (after all, he stood more than a foot taller than I), and there I sobbed as if my heart would break. Which well it might—for it carried a double burden.

Not only was I being parted from my fang-mate—with all the emotional turmoil that carries—but even though Dag loved me as a sister, a role I had tacitly accepted, my true feelings toward him were anything but sisterly. I not only loved Dag, I was in love with him!

Dag, of course, was still in love with Brekka, the now-dead giantess who perished saving his life, and who had been assigned by Odin to be Dag's *hamingja*, his guardian spirit who sometimes visits him in his dreams. It's hard enough to compete with a memory— harder still with a ghost—but I had had hopes that in time Dag might come to feel about me the way I did about him. Now, with his leaving Alfheim for who knows how long, I was filled not only with fear about his safety but despair over our ever having a normal loving life together. Do you wonder that all I could do for the longest time was bawl my eyes out?

Eventually, I had to stop and pull myself together. When I did, I took Dag's head between my hands and—pulling his face down toward mine—planted a very un-sisterly kiss full upon his lips. Let Dag think about that on his wanderings! Stepping back, I looked up into his eyes and declared: "Now go, since go you must . . . but stay safe and come back to me as soon as you possibly can. If you don't . . . why, why I'll come looking for you if I have to follow your trail to the very Gates of Hel. I swear I will!"

"There won't be a day I don't think about you—and miss you— dear Aelas. And I vow that I will return to you." Then Dag turned and headed down the pass, the frisky Ledgi prancing around him and looking back at us from time to time to see why we weren't following them. My Darra whined in sympathy but obediently remained by my side. Just before a bend in the trail carried Dag and Ledgi out of sight, he looked over his shoulder and gave us a final wave. One step more, and all that remained to us were our memories. A new phase in all our lives had just begun.

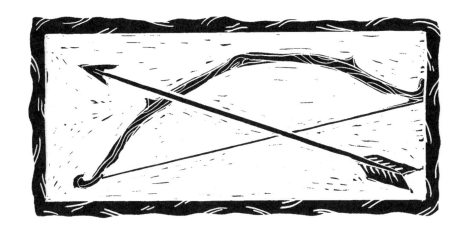

HEART OF A HAWK

Following Dag's departure from Alfheim, it was a subdued party that turned back from the pass into the Alfmark and began the long trek to our village. Both Uncle Formindar and I were dispirited by Dag's forced exile from our midst, and my dog-companion, Darra—seemingly taking her cue from our emotions—contented herself with pacing quietly between us, rather than bounding about excitedly as she usually did.

Our somber mood persisted until the last night of our return journey, when something happened that demanded our full attention. We had intended to camp among the grove of birch trees where we had shared an evening meal, but the wind began to pick up alarmingly and we started to hear the rumble of distant thunder.

Uncle Formindar abruptly stood up and sniffed the air. "There is a really big storm on its way, Aelas. We need to find shelter as soon as possible."

Fortunately, a sizeable rock outcropping could be seen through the trees and, when we reached it a few minutes later, it proved to have several overhangs deep enough to provide us with shelter from the worst effects of the approaching storm—assuming that there was no major shift in the direction of the wind. Needless to say, we checked carefully for troll sign . . . no point in jumping out of the storm and into a stew pot! Our luck held, however, for there was no evidence that trolls had ever occupied this particular refuge.

The storm was not long in arriving. The winds grew so loud that conversation became all but impossible. Thor must have been trying to intimidate a whole army of giants and trolls—or so it seemed— for the rumble of thunder and crack of lightning bolts was almost continuous and nearly deafening. Darra was terrified and added to the cacophony with her howls and yowls. All this commotion went on for what seemed like hours on end. Needless to say, sleep was impossible, and dawn—which saw the storm pass by toward the borderlands—found us fatigued, if at least reasonably dry.

We emerged from beneath our rock shelter to behold a scene of incredible devastation. Surely Ragnarök must have been unleashed upon the forests of Alfheim! Broken limbs lay everywhere, many tree trunks had been snapped off as if struck by the club of a rampaging giant, and here and there we even saw whole trees that had been uprooted. The forests would heal over time, but the scars on the landscape would remain visible for years to come.

I had never before seen anything like this storm damage, and I was shocked beyond words. Even Uncle Formindar, that tower of serenity, was visibly shaken by the extent of the destruction. After silently surveying the scene for several minutes, he let out a deep sigh and exclaimed: "There is naught we can do here, my dear, to replace what is lost or restore the balance. Nature will have to do that for itself. But our help may well be needed back in our village, which surely will not have come through that storm unscathed. Let us hope for the best, and make haste to return there as quickly as we can."

We started off immediately. Had we been able to lope along the trail we had taken on our way to the border with Dag, we might have been able to reach the village in a few hours. However, having to wend our way around or over the obstacles the storm had deposited on the trail rendered our pace painfully slow. Filled with anxiety as I was about the safety of my mother and father—as well as the other members of our village—it was all I could do not to vent my frustration on the universe. Fortunately, Dag's dragon's fang amulet that hung around my neck reminded me to calm down and stay focused on the task at hand.

It was at this point that Darra turned aside from the tortuous path we had been following and commenced barking in her imperative tone that I had learned meant: "Hey, come over here, I've found something important!" No elf who has any claim to wisdom will ignore what her dog is trying to tell her, so despite the urgency of our mission, Uncle Formindar and I paused to learn what Darra had discovered.

My dog was nosing about a large pile of sticks that lay partially crushed beneath the top of a tree that had been snapped off its trunk and had fallen to the ground. As my uncle and I drew near, we could see that it was a nest of some sort. Alas, we could also see that the nestlings it contained had been crushed when the nest was destroyed.

But, wait . . . . Darra was focusing on a feathery bundle that had not been trapped in the wreckage of the nest and was very much alive. It was a goshawk, our tribe's totem bird! Still too young to be able to fly, the hawklet spread its wings, fluffed out its feathers to look as imposing as possible, and opened its beak while hissing loudly. Darra was clearly impressed by the display and kept her distance.

My uncle and I could only chuckle aloud . . . and what a relief it was to have something to laugh about on this otherwise miserable day.

"My, what a fierce young rascal you are," I told the little hawk, which just seemed to glare at me in response. "Whatever is going to become of it, Uncle? I fear that its parents abandoned the area after the nest was destroyed—if they even survived the storm—and this hawklet isn't able to feed itself yet."

"It is imperative that we get back to our village as quickly as possible—my skills as a healer may be needed. Yet my heart goes out to this little one. It has survived so much havoc and loss already in its young life that I feel moved to give it a chance for a full life. And, perhaps, in bonding with this goshawk I can help not only Raiko—as I now name him, for I sense he is a male—but also fill the void in my own life left by the death of Linu, my dog-companion."

My uncle detached his cloak and, stepping forward, deftly tossed it over the young hawk before scooping the bird up in his arms in such a way that it couldn't use beak or talons on Formindar. Tucking the living bundle under one arm, my uncle turned to me and said: "Now, we really must be on our way. I'm sure Raiko will calm down shortly, and I can find some food for him as soon as we get home. A softened strip of dried deer meat should be just the thing for our young friend."

The inconvenience of carrying Raiko may have slowed us down somewhat, but I did not begrudge my uncle the chance to fill the hole left by Linu's death and—if truth be told, though he had left it unsaid—the indefinite absence of his sworn-brother, Dag. Sharing that loss as I did, I could also share in his pain . . . and we could only guess what other losses might yet face us when we reached home.

But, Frey be praised, no storm deaths in our village had been woven into the Norns' Tapestry of Wyrd that day. Several of the elevated storage huts had fallen over—their support poles snapped off by the force of the winds—and there were no tent covers to be seen for they all had been blown away, but our family and friends were whole even if soaked to the bone. So as bad as things were, they could have been so much worse.

Already some members of each family were spreading out clothing and bedding on bushes to dry in the sunshine, while others combed what was left of the forest downwind in the hope of finding the missing tent covers. As soon as we had determined that my parents were unharmed—and reassured them of our well-being—Uncle Formindar handed me the still-bundled little goshawk, Raiko, and went off to check on the other villagers.

Luckily, my family's storage hut had withstood the force of the wind and was still standing. While my mother, Falan, gently held Raiko and crooned reassuringly to calm him down, I scrambled up the notched pole ladder to the hut door and, entering, cut off a chunk of dried deer meat with my dragon-bone hunting knife. After climbing back down, I sliced off a thin strip of meat and chewed it in my own mouth until it was soft enough to offer to Raiko. At first he was so busy squawking that he didn't seem to recognize the deer meat as food, but once he chomped down on the first piece with his beak, he greedily gulped it down and immediately demanded more—loudly and insistently.

Such a voracious feeder was Raiko that it took both my mother and me chewing meat continuously to keep up with him. Eventually, however, even a half-starved little goshawk will eat his fill, and when Raiko had had enough he subsided with a contented little "gleep" and soon fell asleep.

Fortunately my uncle returned by the time of Raiko's next feeding, which he took over . . . save for some of the meat-softening chore. Had Formindar not been able to do so, there would have been a real risk that Raiko might have bonded with me rather than with him.

As the days of summer passed, I spent more time in the woods with Darra hunting for fresh meat for my extended family—furred, feathered, and elvish. Darra would flush our prey, be it hare or grouse, and I would usually bring it down with a well-placed arrow. When seeking larger game, such as red deer, I would recruit another elf—usually my father, Skuttar—as a hunting partner. Strong as I am, carrying a whole deer by myself all the way to the village from miles away would have been a daunting task. Yet to discard any part of one's prey would have been an unthinkable waste, as well as being disrespectful to the animal that had been killed.

When the carcass had been properly skinned in the village, the edible flesh and entrails were removed, the antlers and bones that could be made into tools were carefully set aside, and what little remained was fed to our dogs. My partner and I shared equally in the bounty of our combined efforts.

It may seem strange to outsiders that my father and I would need to divide our game in such a way, for if they are not elves themselves they probably assume that everything is going into a common pot . . . but such is not the case. The clan system that exists in elvish society dictates that familial descent is traced through the mother's line—not the father's. Thus a male's first responsibility is to provide for his sister and her children rather than his wife and hers. Not that Father would have let Mother and me starve, but we really are Formindar's responsibility first and foremost.

My uncle is a wonderful person, but he is a wizard and healer, after all, and is less focused on hunting and trapping than most male elves. Father and Mother were aware of this when they married, so as soon as I was old enough to draw back a bowstring, Skuttar took the time to teach me how to shoot and how to hunt. His sister raised no objections for she appreciated my uncle's unique role in our village and didn't feel Skuttar was neglecting her children by spending more time with me than would have been the custom. Thus I came to be almost as good an archer as my father and, in the process, the principal provider of meat for my mother's tent . . . and for Formindar's as well, when he chose not to eat with us.

✦━《《(∞)》》•⊗•《《(∞)》》━✦

While I was training Darra to be an effective and reliable hunting partner, Formindar was bonding with the rapidly growing Raiko.

21

So complete did this bond become by the time the goshawk was capable of independent flight and killing his own prey, that soon my uncle could communicate with Raiko mind-to-mind. Formindar would picture what he wanted—be it to attack an animal or refrain from eating his own prey once he had killed it—and Raiko would do as he was asked.

The first task was easy, Formindar later confessed to me, for it simply coincided with the goshawk's natural inclinations. More difficult by far was convincing Raiko to voluntarily relinquish his prey. That ran counter to all his instincts, and it was only after he began to develop a growing trust in his elvish partner that Raiko would withdraw his talons from the body of the dead animal without an angry display of wing-spreading, beak-clacking, and loud hissing. But that trust did come and, in time, Raiko and my uncle became inseparable. Formindar had a re-enforced leather patch sewed onto the left shoulder of each of his tunics so Raiko could perch there comfortably whenever the elf went a-walking.

With his short, powerful wings and great agility, Raiko could fly remarkably fast even through fairly dense forest. Add to this his fierce disposition, and very few birds or hares could elude Raiko's attack once he had spotted them. Those that had the sense to "freeze" in place, however, were often overlooked by the goshawk, who relied on his keen eyesight to detect the movement of prey.

"I think I know how to solve that problem, Uncle," I remarked one evening after Formindar had told me of Raiko's "blind spot."

"What do you have in mind, Aelas?"

"If you think that Raiko would tolerate having Darra and me join you, I suggest that the four of us go hunting together tomorrow. Then I can show you my idea."

"I'll make sure he understands he needs to mind his manners. But you and Darra have been a part of his life since the day we first found him, so I can't imagine he would make a fuss now. What about Darra?"

"Oh, Darra will do what I tell her. She's a good dog!" Darra looked up at the sound of her name and pushed her head under my hand so I could scratch that favorite spot between her ears.

"Well, it's settled then," affirmed Formindar. "We'll head out at dawn."

When we drew near a clump of bushes whence in the past Darra had rarely failed to flush a grouse, I spoke to my uncle: "If any grouse are in those bushes, they'll lie low in the hope that we'll walk on past and fail to notice them. I'm going to send Darra in there to scare them out. If any are there, they'll come out in a hurry and fly up into those spruce trees over yonder . . . so you'd better move Raiko from you shoulder to your gloved hand for a quicker take-off."

Formindar nodded and did as I suggested, mind-speaking to the goshawk as he did so. Raiko cocked his head alertly and partially crouched, as I spoke to my dog: "Find the birds, Darra. Go on, girl."

Darra must have already scented our prey for she made a bee-line toward one side of the bushes. A cock grouse exploded skyward, but before it could cover half the distance to the protection of the nearest spruce, Raiko hit the grouse and bore it to the ground. From a view to a kill was as quick as that!

Formindar whistled. "To think that Raiko and I might have passed by and not even known that grouse was there. What a hunting team he and Darra make! We should have no trouble now getting all the small game our family needs . . . and spend much less time doing so. Well done, Aelas!"

I grinned and silently basked in his praise as I knelt to hug Darra, who seemed to sense that she had done something good. Formindar, in turn, stroked Raiko's feathers and talked quietly to him as he restored the goshawk to his perch on my uncle's shoulder.

So successful was our hunting technique that we soon had to travel farther afield so as not to overhunt the populations of game near our village. Thus it was that one brisk, colorful fall day found us at the edge of the fens of Maras, where Dag and I had shared the perils of the Great Hunt on Midsummer's Day. For a moment my thoughts turned again to my wandering fang-mate, and I let out a sigh. *Where was he now? Was he well? Did he miss me as much as I missed him?* I sighed again, then turned back to the matters at hand.

Raiko had brought down several brace of ducks and a loon. The latter was killed despite Formindar's attempt to dissuade the hawk, for elves consider loons to be set apart from all other birds. It is said by some that their haunting calls are the voices of elves who have suffered an agonizing death, and whose souls are trapped in the bodies of loons. Whether true or not, this is the reason that elves won't eat the flesh of loons.

Formindar asked me to dig a shallow grave for the loon's body, but before we interred it my uncle used his hunting knife to carefully remove the loon's beak and several of its wing feathers.

"Why did you do that, Uncle Formindar?"

"A loon's beak has magical properties, Aelas. Properly prepared, it can be fashioned into an arrow point that is proof against any spell that can turn aside iron. When we return home, I'll prepare this one for you; then you can bind it to a shaft and fletch the arrow with the loon's feathers."

"I'm sure it would make an interesting curiosity to hang up in Mother's tent, Uncle, but when would I ever have need of such an arrow? We of the Muorra never use iron arrowheads anyway, so how would a loon's beak be any better than our points of bone or antler?"

Formindar gave me a sage smile. "I'm sure I cannot answer either of your questions, my dear. It is not given to any of us to know the future . . . but when the time is right for the arrow to be used, you will know it—of that I am certain. Until then, keep it safe in your quiver."

I was not well contented with his rather cryptic response, but realizing that my uncle had said all he intended to say at this time, I wisely let the matter drop.

The next day found us traversing the high country that lies between the fens and our village. We had as many birds as we could carry comfortably dangling from our belts, but I was still hopeful of downing a deer we could tote back on a pole.

Suddenly, as we rounded a massive moss-covered boulder, we came upon a large female brown bear that was fattening itself with ripe blueberries as it prepared for hibernation and the birth of its cubs. The bear was as startled as we were and reared up on its haunches to see who the intruders were. Formindar and I immediately began a deliberate, but hasty, retreat—and all might have gone well—but Darra, who had never seen a bear before, ran toward it while barking loudly.

The bear roared and took a swing at Darra with one of its huge paws, the claws coming so close that they ruffled the dog's fur. Darra heeded the message and, yelping, dashed away from the bear . . . and straight toward us!

Now thoroughly annoyed, the bear dropped onto all four legs and charged . . . which is when everything seemed to happen at once. Raiko launched himself from Formindar's shoulder and flew directly at the face of the charging bear, which he raked with his talons before rising into a tight bank so he could renew the attack. Startled, and smarting from the slashes it had sustained, the sow bear braked to a halt and reared up once more so it could use its claws to defend itself. Fearing for Raiko's life should the bear succeed in striking the hawk, I quickly nocked an arrow and—drawing back my bowstring—prepared to plant the shaft deep within the bear's chest.

"Avert!" shouted my uncle, thrusting out his hands to form a pair of three-fingered *algiz* runes. The right hand he held palm-upright toward the bear and Raiko, and the left hand palm-downward and sideways toward me. The results of his action were startling. My arm muscles went limp, the bow sagged in my hand, and I lost my grip on the arrow, which fell to the ground. With an audible "woof" the bear sat down hard on its rump, looking as dazed as if it had run into a tree, while Raiko crash-landed and staggered drunkenly about. Such is the power of the runes!

Formindar addressed the sow bear aloud, although I suspect he was also using mind-speech: "My apologies, Honey Paws, for treating you so rudely . . . but I could not let you hurt my family. The dog meant no harm—she was simply curious—and the hawk only acted to protect us from your attack. I have shown my good will toward you by stopping the elf-maid from shooting you, so if you'll let us depart in peace for our own home, we will leave you to eat your fill of berries without further interruption."

The bear shook her shaggy head for a few moments, as if thinking over what my uncle had said, then grunted, slowly regained her footing, and ambled off.

"Whew," Formindar let out his breath. "I wasn't at all sure how that was going to turn out. Aelas, I have to apologize to you, too, but I had to stop you and the bear—and poor Raiko, too—before anyone was killed or maimed . . . and it all had to happen in the same instant! I know how quick you can be with a bow, and if I had delayed for the second or two it took to spell-cast the bear before telling you to stop, it might have been too late. I just didn't want you to have the death of the bear—and her cubs—on your conscience. Please forgive me."

"Oh, I do, Uncle Formindar, I do. I should have known you wouldn't use a rune spell on me without having an awfully good reason."

My uncle gave me a hug, then gathered up Raiko in his arms and stroked his feathers reassuringly. "I knew you were a fierce hunter, my feathered friend, but it took something like this to show us how fiercely loyal you are as well. How easy it would have been for you to flee the bear's charge, but you stayed and fought to protect us.

You have a great heart, Raiko, and are a true companion."

Restored to Formindar's shoulder, Raiko sat tall and proud—looking as if he had understood my uncle's every word—as our hunting party slowly made its way back to our village without further incident.

Heart of the Sun, Heart of a Dragon

Prologue

Vassai slowly eased over to the edge of the cliff overlooking a deep ravine that was reputed to house a dragon's cave. Yes, there it was . . . and stretched out, resting on a broad, rocky ledge above the opening lay one of the great orms, a huge blue-black female whose slightly sunken sides proclaimed that she had laid a clutch of eggs not long before.

A dragon's egg! thought Vassai. *That would be better by far than stealing a few gold trinkets to arouse the ire of the resident dragon. Not much risk that she'll follow me once I leave the ravine—she'll want to guard the rest of her eggs. But once she alerts her mate, he'll surely come in hot pursuit. Luckily I persuaded the Gammer to fly me from Alfheim to Ormerdal and back again. I'll be long*

*gone before the male dragon ever sets out. He'll know who to blame,
however; the slate-bladed knife I'll "accidentally lose" in the cave
will leave no doubt that the thief is one of the Merin. So off to the
Sea Elf villages he'll fly and give them a good dose of the venomous
cold-fire for which the great orms are so famous.*

Vassai paused for a moment in his internal rant, then resumed:
*And it will serve them right when he does! How dare they exile me?
And for what? "Repeated and flagrant violations of the Alfar Way,"
old Rehalas had said when he pronounced my fate. "By your actions
you have clearly chosen to reject the Light and turn to the Dark. So
be it . . . now the Light rejects you, Vassai. Henceforth you are not a
Light Elf, and you are no longer entitled to live in Alfheim. Gather
your belongings and be on your way by dawn . . . and see that you
never return." May Hel take that pompous old fool . . . may Loki's
daughter take the lot of them! Well, I will have my revenge . . . and
that sooner than later.*

True to his plan, Vassai waited until full darkness had descended,
then he crept as silently as an elf can move—and that is silent,
indeed—down the ravine wall and into the cavern that lay beyond
the portal. Quickly and quietly he removed one of the skull-sized
eggs from atop the dragon's hoard and—almost as an afterthought—
remembered to pick up a golden arm-ring for the Gammer. It was
the payment the great bird had demanded for its services on Vassai's
behalf. Once the egg and arm-ring were safely ensconced in the dark
elf's pouch—and his slate-bladed knife left conspicuously behind—
Vassai slipped back out of the cave and headed off to his meeting
with the Gammer beyond the next ridge.

"Any luck?" rasped the Gammer, peering down its wickedly
curved beak at Vassai as it towered over the dark elf.

"Yes, yes. I got the egg . . . and your golden arm-ring. Now let's
be off before the dragon discovers the theft and sends her mate after
us."

"Even with my beak and talons of iron, I'm no more anxious
than you to meet an angry dragon. So climb on my back and we'll

be on our way." Vassai scrambled to a comfortable position on the Gammer's back, and soon they were aloft and soaring through the night sky toward Alfheim.

Dawn found the great black bird and its passenger over the coastal area that was home to the Merin, and from which Vassai had been exiled by his tribe.

"Bring me down near one of those small coastal ponds that isn't near a Merin village. It wouldn't be good for us to be seen by anyone."

The Gammer promptly banked and glided in to a landing atop a beaver dam in a hanging wetland on the inland side of a great sand dune. Dismounting, Vassai extracted the dragon's egg from his pouch, cast it into the deep pool that lay behind the beaver dam, and watched with satisfaction as the egg sank out of sight.

"Well, that's that. The egg will never be found there, and the father dragon will take his loss out on the Merin villages. Things couldn't be better." Turning toward the Gammer, the dark elf inclined his head in a small bow. "Thank you for your help, Gammer; I couldn't have done all this without you. Perhaps we'll run into each other again some day."

"Aren't you forgetting something, elf? You promised me a gold arm-ring from the dragon's hoard."

"Well, what would you do with an old arm-ring anyway? You don't have any arms. No, I think I'll just hang on to the arm-ring so I'll have something to show for this little adventure."

As Vassai began to sidle away along the beaver dam, he was abruptly seized from behind by a set of huge iron talons. "One does not play that kind of game with the Gammer, elf. With me there is no such thing as a free ride." The dark elf scarcely had time to utter one horrified scream before his head was engulfed by the gaping iron beak of the Gammer and snapped off by a single crunching bite.

The bird dropped the mangled body and almost delicately picked up the pouch with one iron talon. Upending the pouch, he dumped out the arm-ring. Picking the ring up with one foot, the Gammer fastened it around his other leg. After admiring the ring for a moment, the great black bird seized the dark elf's carcass in his talons and carried it off with him into the morning sky to save for a mid-day snack.

Aelas's Tale

Sabmo, the Dark Time—the sunless heart of our long northern winter—is always hard on the Light Elves for, as our name implies, we truly are creatures of light. Nothing so gladdens our hearts as sunlight and the presence of green, growing things. Oh, that is not to say we don't appreciate the muted play of silvery moonlight on the snowscape, or that we fail to be awed by the colorful dance of the *guovsakas* across the northern sky. We are a part of nature, after all . . . but first and foremost, we are the Children of the Light!

The deep snow made hunting more difficult for the forest elves, the Muorra as my tribe is called. We had to rely more heavily on the food we had set aside in our storehouses during the warmer months of the year. These stores dwindled as winter wore on, so belts had to be tightened in order that our food not run out before the spring thaw opened new sources to us.

The winter storms and long period of darkness also meant that we had to spend far more time in the tent than I enjoy doing. Elves are sociable enough—especially with their families—but they also cherish their privacy, and that is not easily attained when sharing tent space with two (my parents, Falan and Skuttar) or three (when Uncle Formindar came by, which was often). I can only do just so much handwork, sing so many songs, and hear so many stories before I'm ready to bolt from the tent into the teeth of a raging blizzard. Be it reasonable or not, mine is a restless spirit! Small wonder I was more than ready for spring to return to Alfheim.

Formindar sensed my disquiet and one afternoon, when I had gone over to his tent to help feed his hawk-friend, Raiko, and to practice the use of protection runes, my uncle broached the subject.

"My dear niece, I cannot help but notice that a sense of *lotkulas* is eluding you these days . . . and that troubles me. Would you like to talk about it?"

Ordinarily, I like to think of myself as being all grown-up and self-reliant, and I would resent outside "interference" that implied otherwise. However, having grown ever closer to my uncle after Dag's departure last summer, I sensed that Formindar truly cared for me and that he was a good listener. So, swallowing my pride, I opened my heart to him and shared all my deepest concerns . . . including one I rarely voiced, even to myself.

"When *is* Dag coming back, Uncle? It has been such a long time since he left us. Do you suppose he could have forgotten us?" I wrung my hands together nervously.

Taking my hands in his, Formindar gazed into my eyes with a look both concerned and somehow calming.

"Dear girl, we both know Dag better than that. He is not one to bestow his heart and his hand lightly. The oath he gave when he and I became sworn-brothers, and the pledge he made when you and he became fang-mates, welled up from the very depths of his being . . . and mere absence would never shake him from those paths, no matter how far away from us Odin's mission leads him. We must trust Dag to remain the same fine fellow we both know and love . . . and trust also that at some time in the future he *will* return to us. I am sure he is as anxious for that day as we are."

"That's all well and good to say, Uncle, but the uncertainty is driving me mad. I can't not think about him, but I know it isn't good for me to sit around and think about him all the time, either. That's just not my nature. I've got to be doing something, to feel as if I have some control over my destiny. If Odin hadn't absolutely forbidden me to follow Dag, I would have been on his trail months ago. Whatever am I to do?"

Formindar smiled his gentle smile, as much with his eyes as his lips. "When an elf becomes restless—for whatever reason—he often wanders off on his own for an extended period of time until he solves, or at least comes to terms with, whatever problem was causing the restlessness. It seems to me, Aelas, that such a period of *manalmas* may be just what you need."

"I'd be willing to try anything that might help. But where would I go on my out-wandering?"

"Have you ever visited the great ocean, along whose shores our cousins the Merin dwell? There are mighty sights to be seen there."

"It sounds fascinating, Uncle. If you could sketch the best route on a strip of birchbark, Darra and I will head off as soon as the weather permits."

"You know," Formindar mused, "it has been a good many years since I last saw the sea, and there is something about it that draws one back. If you wouldn't mind the company, perhaps Raiko and I could join you and point out the way."

Leaping to my feet, I gave Formindar a big hug. "Oh, would you go with me, Uncle? That would make the journey so much more enjoyable."

Formindar grinned. "It's settled then. Let's tell your parents what we intend to do, then we'll leave as soon as enough snow has melted to open the trails to the coast."

⸺⸱⟪⟨⟩⟫⸱⊗⸱⟪⟨⟩⟫⸱⸻

Making preparations for our trek occupied most of my waking hours from thence until the onset of the great spring thaw, and it left me little time or reason to feel sorry for myself. We were, of course, limited to what we could carry on our backs, for even a small sled would be cumbersome in the woods and would have to be abandoned as soon as most of the snow had melted from the trail.

The only things that each of us could take in our skin backpacks were one change of dry clothing and some dried food to sustain us and our animal-companions when fresh food was unavailable. Moreover, each of us would carry a fur-lined bedroll fastened across our shoulders. And, because I was the principal hunter in our group, in

33

addition to my recurved bow and hunting spear, I would be carrying a waterproof dragonskin belt quiver containing a full complement of arrows, a spare bowstring, and a set of spare points.

To be adequately prepared, but not over-burdened with things, is to have little to fear on a journey such as the one my uncle and I faced . . . usually. Somehow life always does manage to challenge us when we least expect it!

Before many more days had passed, I awoke one morning to the cracking of ice and a sound I had not heard since last fall—the tinkle of running water. The great spring thaw had arrived during the night and freed the stream that runs near our village from the grip of the Frost Giants who rule the northern world in winter. Thereafter, the days grew longer as the chariot of the sun spent increasingly more time taking its daily journey across the northern sky. I was not alone among the Children of the Light in welcoming this change. Everyone's spirit was raised, and soon the morning songs of the elves joined those of the increasing number of birds in welcoming back the Light. Spring had returned to Alfheim . . . and it was time that Uncle Formindar and I were on our way to the sea. I could scarcely imagine what it must look like, and I could hardly wait to see—and smell—it for myself!

The trail we followed toward the coast eventually brought us in sight of Stuoravuodna, the Great Fjord, which extends from the sea deep into Alfheim. Its waters are usually far calmer than those of the ocean, and they provide the Merin with much of their livelihood—an abundant and diverse food source as well as a safe and swift avenue of transportation on which they could paddle with their round, seal-skin coracles. Much as I love the inland forest home of our own people, the Muorra, I was left almost speechless by the vista I beheld

"Oh, it's beautiful, Uncle!" I enthused. "The Merin must love it here."

Formindar smiled affably. "On a sunny day like today, when the wind is gentle, there are few places finer. But even the Merin, proud as they are of their homeland, would admit that when the weather turns—and blustery winds from the sea whip the waters of the fjord into a froth—they are quick to beach their coracles and take shelter from the storm that usually follows. And, of course, life is more precarious for those Merin who take their coracles out onto the sea itself in pursuit of their prey . . . or perhaps simply an adventure. The sea is far less forgiving of mistakes than is the fjord—and it is home to much larger predators."

"Oh," I said sheepishly. "I guess even the most beautiful places may hide pitfalls for the unwary."

"Indeed so, my dear, but if you bear that in mind and always remain alert, there is no reason you cannot enjoy the beauty at the same time. Now, I suggest that we head on down to the fjord. With luck we should reach Njalmadak before dusk and be able to avail ourselves of our cousins' hospitality. The Merin are famous for the countless ways in which they can prepare delicious seafood dishes. I'm afraid they will make our forest fare seem rather bland by comparison."

And so it would prove to be, but before the trail had descended much farther, Raiko suddenly launched himself from Formindar's shoulder and soon brought down—in a flurry of black feathers—an unwary crow he had been watching.

"Well," mused Formindar, "it seems we're going to have to wait a bit while Raiko eats his fill. No matter how friendly an animal-companion may be, it is never wise to interrupt a feeding predator unless its prey was killed during a group hunt when it knows it has to share."

Watching Raiko pluck the crow's feathers and cast them aside so he could get at the meat, Formindar suddenly exclaimed: "Ha! I just remembered something." Cautiously approaching Raiko so as not to startle the goshawk and put him on the defensive, my uncle picked up two of the discarded crow feathers, smoothed them out between his fingers, and presented one of them to me.

"There is a saying that wearing a crow's feather brings one good luck in finding things. It has been my experience that one can never have too much good luck, so I suggest we fasten these feathers onto our hoods . . . even if they didn't bring much good luck to the crow!"

The rest of our descent to the shoreline of the fjord was uneventful, but the trail we had been following ended there with no sign of other trails leading along the edge of the steep-sided water body in either direction.

"Now what, Uncle?" I asked perplexedly.

"Be patient," Formindar chuckled, though I failed to see what he found amusing. "Help is already on the way—look!"

Sure enough, as I looked across the waters in the direction he was pointing I espied a coracle approaching. The elf who knelt in it paddled the craft smoothly, singing as he stroked. I could not make out the words of his song until he drew very close to where Formindar and I were standing, so it was clear that his singing reflected his exuberance over being alive rather than an attempt to impress us . . . but I was impressed anyway.

"Well, well," the paddler called out as he brought the coracle right up to the water's edge, "what brings two intrepid travelers from the forests of the Muorra to the brink of Stuoravuodna? You are the first People of the Goshawk—and that is a beautiful hawk you have with you—to visit here since the winter snows began."

"My name is Formindar, and this is my niece, Aelas Falansdottir. We are on an out-wandering, seeking new sights and experiences . . . and hoping for a chance to reflect and restore *lotkulas*. Our immediate concern, however, is how to reach Njalmadak. My good friend Verdi lives there, and she would be glad to host us during our visit."

"Formindar of the Muorra? My own village, Siskebu, lies far up the fjord, but even there we have heard of the Guardian. There is no Merin village in which you would not be welcome. Still, if you are bound for Njalmadak, it would be a great honor for Dattulas son of Tsiwakan to take you there."

The Guardian? My dear old Uncle Formindar? My mind was spinning. *Guardian of what or who?* I had thought I knew him well, but clearly there was far more to my uncle than I had ever suspected.

The eye-twinkling glance Formindar cast in my direction showed that he was well aware of my consternation . . . and was amused by it. Hmph! I promised myself that he and I were going to have a nice long discussion soon, once we could do so privately. But for now, I could only watch as he politely inclined his head toward the Merin and responded to his greeting.

"Your courtesy does honor to your mother, Tsiwakan, and to all the other good folk of Siskebu—may the Light ever shine on your village, Dattulas. I have good memories of the time I spent there . . . and perhaps I shall return some day. Meanwhile, my niece and I would be delighted to accept your kind offer to transport us to Njalmadak. And, since I see a spare paddle in your craft, it is only fair that we help you propel the much heavier load."

Dattulas objected: "It isn't fitting that the Guardian should have to paddle!"

"Oh, it would hardly be a new experience for me," remarked my uncle, "but I actually had Aelas in mind to ply the off-paddle."

"But she's a female!" blurted Dattulas, now thoroughly distressed

"So I've noticed, but you must not let that fact upset you. She is also an experienced paddler who has ably handled a coracle in the Great Hunt. Come, my boy, don't let old notions blind you to new realities."

Abashed, Dattulas stammered an apology, then helped steady his craft while Formindar and I found the places to kneel that would ensure the greatest stability once the coracle was under way. Our task was made more difficult by Darra's insistence on sitting on her haunches so she could keep an eye on everything around her. Raiko, for his part, seemed content to simply perch on my uncle's shoulder as we shoved off into the deep waters of the fjord.

Determined to justify Formindar's declaration of my competence—and to show Dattulas that his concept of what an elf-maid was capable of doing was based on ignorance—I drove my paddle into the water with all the vigor I could muster. Not to be outdone by a mere "female," the Merin put out his best effort as well. Despite the added weight of our party, the coracle seemed to fly across the surface of the fjord, so less than an hour passed before we could see traces of smoke rising from cooking fires in the village of Njalmadak.

When the coracle slid up to the gravel bar below the village, where a number of other coracles rested belly-up, Dattulas hopped out into the gentle surf to steady the craft while the rest of us disembarked. After we had thanked him profusely for his help, Formindar urged him to stay the night rather than having to paddle much of the way back to Siskebu after dark.

"I appreciate the offer, but I promised my mother I'd return this evening. Until she knows I'm safely back, she'll not be able to sleep soundly . . . so go I must. It promises to be a calm, moonlit night, so the paddling shouldn't prove arduous. Give me your blessing, Guardian, and I'll be off."

Formindar traced a journey-rune on the Merin's inclined forehead while intoning: "May your paddle be unbroken, your coracle seams unbreached, your wake straight, and your judgment sound. Travel with the Light, my boy."

Dattulas thanked Formindar, then turned to me: "Aelas Falansdottir, you have shown me that I have a lot to learn. Thank you for teaching me the lesson so graciously. Fare thee well."

Hopping back into his coracle, Dattulas began to paddle up-fjord, pausing only once to give us a final salute with his raised paddle before his image dwindled in the distance. We watched until he disappeared from sight, then Formindar remarked: "The lad has turned out well, indeed. His mother must be very proud of him. Ah, Tsiwakan, Tsiwakan, fairest of the fjord-maidens . . . ." My uncle sighed deeply and turned back toward the village we had come to visit—Njalmadak. The smell of salt in the air, as well as the taste of brine on my lips, told me the village must not be far from the point where the fjord joined the open sea.

Now, what was that all about? I asked myself as we walked toward the lodges that comprised the village. Clearly Formindar had visited Siskebu at some time in the past and had met the mother of Dattulas. She obviously had made quite an impression on him, so it seemed strange that he had never mentioned the encounter back in our village. At least he hadn't done so in my hearing; perhaps he had shared more with his sister and fang-mate, my mother, Falan. Still, curious as I was, I had learned enough of the Alfar Way to realize that my uncle was entitled to keep his private thoughts private until—and unless—he chose to share them. But, oh my goodness, I was finding hidden nooks and crannies in Formindar's past that I had never dreamed existed!

When we came at last to the lodge of Formindar's friend Verdi, who—it turned out—was the head-woman of the village, we were warmly greeted, indeed. The site of village councils, Verdi's whale-ribbed lodge was larger than the others in Njalmadak so it could seat the heads of all the family groups that lived in the village. Indeed, after feeding us a bewildering array of the most delicious seafood dishes I had ever tasted—and not forgetting a share for Darra and Raiko—our hostess convened a council meeting on the spot, not only to introduce me to the village leaders, most of whom already knew my uncle, but to lay before him a serious problem that the Merin had been facing since the previous fall.

"It is good that the Light has drawn you here, Guardian. I was just about to send messengers to the forests of the Muorra to ask for your assistance."

"I am glad that my arrival is timely, my friend, but whatever is the matter?"

"The leaves had not yet fallen from the trees on the ridges when we were paid a very agitated visit by the great orm Aratak. It seems that an egg had been stolen from the nest of his mate, Valdai . . . stolen apparently by one of the Merin or, more likely, by someone wishing to cast suspicion on the Merin."

"That's awful!" gasped Formindar. "Who in his right mind would steal a dragon's egg to begin with? He couldn't very well expect to hold it for ransom—much as the great orms prize their offspring, they would not tolerate being forced to "buy" one back—and their vengeance would be both swift and final.

"Assuming for the moment that the thief wanted the egg for himself—to hatch and raise the dragonet—how could he possibly hope to keep the creature's existence a secret once it began to grow? It certainly couldn't happen in any elvish community, so I think it safe to conclude that none of the Merin took the egg. Why did Aratak think that your people might be responsible?"

"Because," Verdi responded, "a slate-bladed knife, which only the Merin make, was found near the nest where the thief had dropped it—either accidentally or on purpose."

"Deliberately, I would wager, Verdi. Yes, now I see why you think the thief was trying to cast blame on the Merin . . . although why he would do so eludes me. What could he hope to gain by stirring up enmity between the great orms and the Merin?"

"Well," opined the head-woman, "at least he failed in that regard, if such was his intention. When Valdai summoned Aratak to pursue the thief and bring back their missing egg, she was beside herself with grief and rage—and, no doubt, some guilt over not having prevented the theft in the first place. She ordered Aratak to swoop down on the Merin villages along the coast and spray them with his venomous cold-fire until the terrified elves surrendered the egg and the thief.

"Aratak told us that he was equally enraged by the theft, and when he left the nest cave he fully intended to do exactly what Valdai had demanded. However, during the flight from Ormerdal to the Alfheim coast he had time to calm himself and think more carefully about the circumstances. When he did so, he came to the same conclusion that you did and realized that the thief was trying to trick him into attacking the Merin and perhaps provoking an elf-orm war. So, when he arrived at the coast, instead of unleashing his cold-fire upon us, the great silver dragon asked for our help in finding his egg and, if possible, the thief.

"We willingly agreed to do so, of course, both because he and his mate deserve our help, but also because we want to 'have a few words' with the person who bears us so much ill will. I sent messengers up the great fjord to all the Merin villages along it—even distant Siskebu—to talk with the villagers in council, asking them for information and advice . . . and encouraging them to send out search parties to seek throughout the lands they know the best. Alas, none had seen or heard anything unusual, and then the early snows brought a halt to active searching for the winter. With the spring thaw, we have begun again and are expanding the search to include the seacoast as well, even though there are far fewer permanent villages there than along the fjords and rivers leading to the coast."

"My niece and I would be glad to join in the search," my uncle declared, "and will be ready to do so in the morning. Should we be fortunate enough to find the egg, how do we get word to Aratak?"

Verdi responded: "He continues to fly back and forth over the land of the Merin, searching the terrain below with his keen dragon-sight, so he is never very far away. Should you find the egg, use one of these wands to cast a need-rune skyward . . . and Aratak will come." Verdi extracted a polished, hand-length sliver of sea-dragon rib from her sleeve and handed it to Formindar, who acknowledged the gift with a nod.

41

The coast of Alfheim is marked not only by expanses of sandy beaches and low-shelving rock outcrops that permit exploration on foot, but also by long stretches of sheer, rugged cliffs that do not. Thus we accepted Verdi's kind offer of a coracle that would permit us to paddle along the coast to the south of Njalmadak. This allowed us to skirt the unscalable cliffs, then beach the coracle to explore the areas that could be traversed by foot. Each evening we would pull the coracle well above the high-tide line and, upending our craft, crawl beneath it to spend the night protected from wind and sea-spray. Wrapped in our elven cloaks—woven as they were from magically enhanced spider silk—we were warm enough despite the cool night air. For, indeed, winter was not yet so far in the past that we could not see an occasional small ice floe drifting past, broken loose from the melting pack ice far to the north.

Despite sending Raiko out for several hours each day to lend an extra pair of eyes, as well as give our search a different, higher viewscape, by the third day we had found nothing and I was becoming increasingly discouraged that we ever would. The fact that the weather, which had been sunny for the first two days, had become overcast and gray added to my bad mood.

"What's the point of going any farther, Uncle? There are so many cracks and crevices that egg could be hidden in where we would never see it. Or maybe the thief simply buried it deep in the sand. This is like hunting for a pine needle in a birch forest, or one particular pollywog in a beaver pond. Can't we try something else?"

The next morning brought what my people call a *saisa*, a floe of pack ice that had been driven on shore during the night. We walked around its base, admiring its water-sculpted sides. That was enough exploration of this beached "ice-whale" to satisfy my curiosity about this phenomenon of the northern seas, but Formindar was drawn somehow to clamber up to the top of the floe. There he stood with cloak billowing and arms outstretched as if to greet the spirit of the sea. It was a sight that moved me strangely and one I think I shall not soon forget.

I was startled from my momentary reverie by my uncle's shout: "*Baeive, baeive*! The sun, the sun! Come quickly, Aelas. You must see this."

To hear was to heed, and puzzled as I was by the source of Formindar's excitement—for I could see no sun in the sky—I scrambled up the floe to join him and see for myself. Darra ran about in circles, whining in frustration, for the climb was clearly beyond her ability.

"What is it?" I cried. "Surely you haven't found the dragon's egg atop an ice floe fresh from the sea?"

"Oh, no," he chuckled, "but with this kind of luck, I have to believe that our search is favored by the Light . . . and that Valdai's precious egg cannot elude us much longer. Look!"

Formindar pointed to the ice at his feet where a throbbing golden light emerged from a small circular hole in the frozen surface. Kneeling, he carefully reached into the hole and reverently extracted the source of the light, an elongate, pointed orange stone rife with sparkling flecks of gold.

"It is a *baeive-njuolla*," my uncle uttered in a low tone, "a 'sun-arrow.' They are believed by some to be living sun beams sealed in rock to serve the Light. Whatever the truth of the matter, a 'sun-arrow' is a source of great power in the hands of an elvish wizard, and I feel gifted beyond my worth to have been led to this one."

"Not every wizard has one, then?"

"Oh my, no," my uncle replied. "They truly are as rare as your special pollywog in a beaver pond."

"Do you think, perhaps, that your lucky crow feather might have had something to do with finding it?"

"Hmm. That idea really hadn't occurred to me, but I couldn't rule it out. The power of the Light can be manifested in a myriad of ways."

"Well, if it were true, do you suppose a crow's feather could help us find the dragon's egg?"

"Indeed, it might," opined Formindar, "and since the idea is yours, to your feather goes the honor of attempting the task."

Pleased to have contributed a good suggestion, I promptly removed the feather from my hood and handed it to my uncle. Holding it aloft in one hand, he traced a finding-rune above it with the other while he intoned a magic charm:

> *"Feather fly and find the path,*
> *To dragon's egg, not dragon's wrath;*
> *Reveal the fate of Valdai's young,*
> *In latter days your deed be sung."*

A small whirlwind began to form directly above the feather in Formindar's outstretched hand and, in the twinkling of an eye, it swept the feather upward in an ever-widening gyre until that small black object sailed inland over the giant sand dune and out of our sight. My uncle was quick to send the goshawk after it, calling out: "Hai, Raiko, aloft and follow."

We waited with bated breath for Raiko's return because we had no idea how far the feather would travel before alighting. Fortunately, it was not more than a few minutes—though it seemed much longer—before Raiko returned to Formindar's shoulder in an impressive swoop. The two of them carried on a brief conversation mind-to-mind, then my uncle turned to me and spoke.

"Our good luck holds, Aelas . . . and you won't believe where the feather has landed. Raiko showed me a thought picture of a sizeable beaver pond, of all things, that lies in a wetland area just beyond the great dune. Let's walk up to the top of the dune and see what there is to be seen."

Even accustomed as my uncle and I were to hill climbing elsewhere, we found the soft, yielding sand of the high dune challenging, indeed. It even slowed Darra down a bit, much to her apparent surprise. Yet top it we eventually did, there to gaze down upon a tranquil pond whose waters were held back by a lengthy beaver dam, near which sat the builder's lodge.

"If the egg was dropped into the pond last fall, Uncle, wouldn't the young dragon have died in the shell soon thereafter?"

"I'm sure you are right, Aelas. But there is one way the dragonet might—and I do say *might*—still be alive and hidden in the pond. And, if I am right, we should be able to find the feather shortly, and save ourselves a hike around the entire pond."

"Don't keep me in suspense, Uncle Formindar. What are you thinking?"

"Assuming that the thief had no intention of ever coming back to reclaim the egg, and only stole it to stir up trouble, he may well have simply dumped it in the pond to prevent its rescue and—at the same time—remove the evidence of his guilt. But what if the egg was discovered before it was too late and moved to a place of safety in the pond where it would be out of the water, hmm? What do you think of that possibility?"

"Moved by whom? And where would there be a safe place that would be both *in* the pond and *out* of the water?" I let my eyes scan the length and breadth of the pond once more—and then the answer hit me. "Oh, of course. Only the inside of the beaver lodge fits that description. But are you suggesting that a beaver found the egg and pushed it up into the lodge above the water level?"

"Prompted by some instinct I cannot begin to fathom, I think that is exactly what a beaver may have done. Shall we go down there now and see if we are right?" And without waiting for my response, Formindar headed down the back side of the dune toward the beaver dam.

When we reached the point on the dam nearest the lodge, my uncle triumphantly pointed at the crow feather proudly standing erect like a banner, its quill embedded in the top of the lodge. "It seems almost certain now that the egg is here, but the only way we will know for sure is to open the lodge. Since neither of us has the skill to do that without destroying the beaver's hard work, I'm going to use some runic magic to first open a hole in the top of the lodge and then rebind it once the egg has been removed—assuming it is there, of course."

He waded out to the lodge, knelt atop it, and—signing the proper runes—chanted the following:

> *"Open wide the beaver's hut,*
> *The dragon's egg reveal;*
> *Once the egg is taken out,*
> *The lodge roof soon reseal."*

The branched dome of the lodge appeared to unweave itself in the blink of an eye. Formindar reached within the opening, gingerly raised the egg out of its sanctuary, and cradled it in his arms while the branches rewove themselves to cap the lodge, which now looked as if it had never been disturbed.

"Do you think the little dragon is still alive in the egg, Uncle?" I asked anxiously.

Wading back from the lodge to the dam, Formindar knelt beside me and carefully nested the egg on the cloak I had removed and laid upon the dam.

"I don't smell an odor of decay, Aelas, so there is a good chance that it still lives. Let me listen a moment for a heartbeat." Placing his right ear against the leathery surface of the egg, my uncle was silent for a time but then began to muse: "I can detect some feeble body movement and sense a faint, irregular heartbeat. But this is the time of the year that over-wintering dragon eggs usually hatch, so the movements of a hatchling-to-be should be extremely vigorous as it struggles to free itself from the egg. I fear that the heart-fire of this poor little one burns very low. The warmth provided by the hibernating beavers may have been enough to keep the baby dragon alive . . . but not enough to let it develop normally. Alas, now that the time has come for it to hatch, it doesn't seem to have the strength to break out of the egg."

"Oh, no! Can't we do something? Couldn't Aratak do something if he were here? Hurry and summon him!"

"I don't know what he could do . . . and besides, there is no time to spare. Either we act now and do what we can, or this poor little one will be dead by sunset. It may not survive anyway, but I would far rather try and fail than sit back and let nature take its course . . . and wonder ever after if I could have made a difference."

Filled with a sudden insight, I blurted: "That's what being the Guardian is all about, isn't it . . . doing all you can to protect Alfheim and all who live here?"

Formindar smiled: "That is certainly a large part of it, my dear, but we'll have to save that discussion for a less hectic occasion. What we have to do now is to remove that egg shell without harming the dragonet. First, I'll use my dragon-bone knife to make a shallow cut through the leathery surface from end to end. Then, while I pull the sides apart, if you'll slip your hands into the opening and under the body, it shouldn't be too difficult to carefully remove the dragonet. Once it's been dried off on the cloak, we will be able to see what we have to deal with."

I followed Formindar's instructions to the letter, and it was only a few moments later that I anxiously held out a flaccid, gray, and weakly struggling dragonet for his inspection.

"Oh, dear, he really *is* in bad shape! His heart-fire has burned so low that it is about to flicker out. Too bad, too bad. And yet . . . ."

"What is it, Uncle? Have you thought of some way to save him?"

"One chance I see, and it must come now!" he cried and cast a spell of unconsciousness on the hatchling. Carefully laying the now limp body of the dragonet on its back, Formindar drew his dragon-bone knife—the only kind that could penetrate dragon hide—and cut a long opening in the body wall to expose the chest cavity. Extracting the throbbing "sun-arrow" from his pouch, he carefully inserted the stone into the wall of the dragonet's feebly and erratically beating heart. Almost at once the heart began to take on the steady rhythm of the sunstone, and to beat ever more strongly as well. Formindar cast some bind runes that first sealed the stone permanently in place, then reclosed the body wall without leaving so much as a scar. I had heard that my uncle was a great healer, but what he did this day was truly extraordinary!

But more surprises were yet to come. As we watched in amazement, the deathly gray pallor of the dragonet's scales faded away to be replaced by a rich orange color highlighted by flecks of gold that glittered in the sunlight. It was as if the little fellow's scales had taken on the complexion of the "sun-arrow" itself. And, no sooner had Formindar removed the effect of the rune of unconsciousness, than the dragonet rolled over on his belly, struggled to a sitting position, and gazed curiously at each of us.

"Oh, my," breathed my uncle, for once at a loss for words.

"It's a miracle, Uncle Formindar," I gasped. "You've truly performed a wonder that far surpasses belief."

"Miracle, indeed, Aelas . . . but not of my making. Mine were but the hands—the power was in the stone—so credit the miracle to the Light that sustains us all, and of which this little fellow now seems to be a living symbol.

"Now it is high time we let his anxious father know the good news. I don't know how long it will take Aratak to get here once he sees the runic signal, so you might want to catch some crickets or grasshoppers for the dragonet to munch on while he waits. After what he has been through, I daresay he has a right to be hungry."

Formindar drew the wand that Verdi had given to him, and he cast a glowing dragon bind-rune high in the sky where it hung like a beacon to guide Aratak to us. Meanwhile, insects were abundant near the beaver pond so I had no difficulty providing an ample offering to our scaly little charge. Instead of simply grabbing them in his mouth as a baby bird would have done, he insisted on grasping each one in a forefoot, lifting the insect up where he could inspect it, and then solemnly popping it into his mouth.

"Look at what fine manners he has, Uncle. He will truly be a prince among dragons."

Formindar laughed merrily, then suddenly looked up as a dragon-shaped shadow blocked the sun from our view. Aratak the Invincible had arrived! Elves, being magical beings themselves, are not easily overawed, but the biggest dragon I had ever seen up close was the fen-orm Dag and I had slain on our Great Hunt the previous year. It was impressive enough—especially when it swam toward me with jaws agape—but silvery Aratak was easily twice as long, and before he folded his huge batlike wings he was—yes, I'll say it—simply awesome! Uncle Formindar took all this magnificence in stride, however, merely bowing to Aratak and then standing aside to direct the dragon's attention to his newly discovered offspring.

"I believe this young fellow belongs to you, Aratak."

The great orm cocked his head to peer at the dragonet, then poked his snout down to sniff at it. "He certainly s-s-smells-s-s like one of mine," Aratak conceded, "but there has-s-s never been a golden dragon in our line before. How very puz-z-zling."

Formindar smiled and told Aratak the whole story as it had unfolded, concluding by saying: "So you can see that you and Valdai have a very special dragonet here, Aratak. I cannot read the future with great confidence, but I would not be at all surprised if he was not saved to serve the Light for some great purpose yet to be revealed."

"S-s-so it would s-s-seem to me als-s-o, dragon-friend, and to that end I will call him S-s-suonjar, S-s-sunbeam, and rais-s-se him to s-s-serve the Light, which has-s-s already s-s-set its-s-s claim upon him."

"Well said, Aratak, well said. An apt name and a worthy pledge. I look forward to hearing great things of Suonjar as he grows into maturity."

"That you shall, Formindar. Valdai and I owe you and your niec-c-ce a debt of gratitude we can never repay. S-s-still, for what it is-s-s worth, keep the wand and should either of you ever need my help, cas-s-st the dragon bind-rune into the s-s-sky . . . and Aratak *will* come."

With that final farewell to us both, Aratak gently gathered his newfound son into one curled forefoot before leaping skyward and, after saluting us with one dip of his great wings, soaring back home to Valdai with their precious golden treasure.

Epilogue

Despite their concerns, the elves never did learn who had stolen the dragon's egg. When word of Vassai's exile spread from one Merin village to another, there were questions about his possible involvement. But, unbeknownst to the villagers, Vassai was no longer in any condition to confirm their suspicions.

As for the Gammer, he had already put his role in the theft behind him and flown back to his aerie high in the most remote mountains of the Alfmark. From there he will venture forth each evening to menace the lives of reindeer, and to haunt the dreams of elves and humans alike.

HEART OF A DWARF

Uncle Formindar's and my adventures among the Merin —with the eventual rescue of the baby golden dragon, Suonjar—quelled my restlessness and eased, for a time, the ache in my heart for my exiled fang-mate, Dag. But, as usual, the ensuing winter—with its necessary constraints on outdoor activities—caused my spirits to sink once more. Finding me in such a mood one day, my uncle suggested another expedition for the two of us and our animal companions.

"We could explore the high fjell this time. What say you, Aelas? We'll cross the great plateau, play 'rump tag' with the reindeer herds, and follow Spring right up to the edge of the craggy mountains. There we'll drink the coldest water you've ever tasted from glacier-fed freshets, as well as breathe air so clean and clear that I swear you'll be able to see farther than you have ever seen before. As for adventures, as well you know, they rarely happen to those who never stir from their tents . . . but if you set off with open eyes and heart, why who knows when something strange and wondrous will cross your path . . . or you, its! So, what think you, my dear? Shall we plan a visit to Varrai, the land of the Duodda—the People of the Gyrfalcon?"

After that description, how could I possibly refuse to go? Not that I wanted to decline his offer, for exploring previously unvisited parts of Alfheim seemed to be just the thing to occupy my mind and raise my spirits.

Our preparations were much the same as they had been when we set off to visit the Merin the previous year, except that then we had been heading down into the advancing Spring, and this time we would be following it up into the mountains—where reprovisioning might prove challenging. This factor made it necessary for us to delay our departure until Spring had fully arrived in the forests of Vuobmai, as our part of Alfheim is called.

So it was that we headed out from our village up through the towering evergreen forests of Vuobmai until they gave way to the shorter black-and-white-barked birches, and we finally emerged above and beyond the tree-line. By doing so we had truly departed from Vuobmai and entered Varrai, the realm of the mountain elves— the Duodda.

Having been accustomed to the varied sounds of the forest all my life—and in the past year, the constant yammering of gulls and crash of waves along the sea coast—I had been expecting the high fjell to be a place of deep silence, but I was mistaken. The air, it seemed, was in constant motion, breathing and sighing, whispering and moaning—truly the voices of the mountains. The unrelenting voices I heard on the high fjell seemed to be speaking to me, to warn me, to demand something of me—so after a time I began to long for the relative quiet of my forest home. Still, the clear air and unbroken vistas that enabled a sharp-eyed elf to see almost "to the edge of forever" were awe-inspiring, so I resolved to set aside my prejudices and simply try ignoring the voices in the wind. After all, they didn't seem to bother Uncle Formindar.

We did encounter several reindeer herds in our wanderings, but not wishing to take large game on another tribe's hunting grounds without permission, we confined our hunting to the abundant small game—such as hares and snow grouse—a task in which we were aided by my dog-companion, Darra, and my uncle's goshawk friend, Raiko. The nearly treeless habitat was different from what all four of us were used to hunting in, but we adapted very quickly.

Although Uncle Formindar had once spoken of "playing rump tag" with the reindeer, when the opportunity arose to see if we could stalk close enough to an individual deer to slap it on the rump, we decided against the idea. For one thing, frightening a reindeer for no better reason than one's own amusement hardly seemed respectful to the deer . . . and thus would be contrary to the Alfar Way. Moreover, causing the reindeer to become more skittish around elves didn't seem fair to the Duodda hunters, whose villages depended on them to provide meat for their families and friends

Each evening we camped on the lee side of the most suitable pile of boulders we could find, primarily to provide a windbreak but also to shield our backs in the unlikely event of an attack by a desperately hungry predator or a hostile being of some ilk. Needless to say, we relied heavily on Darra's sharp ears and even keener sense of smell to alert us.

Before turning in for the night, we would gaze in silence at the stars (which seemed more numerous than what we could see from our forest home), tell a story or two, and discuss the meaning of life. It was on such an occasion that I broached a subject which had been tweaking my curiosity for almost a year.

"Uncle, what exactly does it mean when other elves call you the Guardian? Are you the only one? And how were you chosen for that role? You promised me once—when we were hunting for the dragon's egg—that you would tell me when the time was right. Well, I can't imagine a better time than now, nor a better place."

"Nor can I, Aelas, nor can I," responded Formindar with a chuckle. "Now, to begin with, there is only a single Guardian of Alfheim at any one time, and he—for only rarely does the responsibility befall a female elf—is chosen by his predecessor after a long and careful consideration of promising individuals from all parts of Alfheim. The Guardian is charged with maintaining the Balance—in all its aspects—throughout the land, be it through his skills as a healer or his ability to thwart the efforts of the ill-intentioned. The one who is chosen will, of necessity, need to be adept at wizardry . . . but he must always use those powers for the benefit of others, not to enrich himself nor swell his sense of self-pride. Such is the Guardian's *salimus* or *wyrd*, as gods and men would call it."

"Well," I replied, "from what I've seen, your mentor couldn't have made a better choice! You're the gentlest, most compassionate person I know—yet the most decisive in times of crisis."

Formindar's arms enfolded me in a big hug. When he released me, he said: "It does my heart good to know you feel that way, my dear, for I could not love you more if you were my own daughter. But being Guardian has its limitations, you know. I can give advice or deal directly with some situations, but I cannot resolve every problem that may arise in Alfheim . . . regardless of our people's expectations that I can—and should—do so. In pursuing my responsibilities, I tend to wander farther afield and for longer periods of time than most elves do, and this has proved to be a mixed blessing. While it is true that I have had the privilege of exploring Alfheim from one end to the other, I have also not been able to spend nearly as much time with my kinfolk and friends in our village as I would have liked."

"That's right," I observed. "Now that you mention it, I don't remember seeing nearly so much of you in the village before Dag came . . . and since he left, you and I have been spending a lot of time together."

"Indeed," my uncle agreed, "you young people have wrought quite a change in my life over the past several years. Dag's 'education' was, at the least, an implicit charge from Odin All-Father that could have been perilous to disregard . . . even had I not felt so strongly connected to Dag from the day we met by the tarn.

"And you, Aelas, have been a delightful and trustworthy traveling companion with whom to share the adventures we have experienced together since Dag's exile began. Hopefully they have helped to lessen the loneliness you have felt because of his absence . . . as they have for me."

"Oh, Uncle Formindar," I cried, "that's exactly how I feel! If I can't be with Dag, I just need to be doing something useful to make the time pass more quickly . . . and our adventures certainly have done that."

Just then a raspy, high-pitched voice broke in, sounding as if it were coming from the boulder against which I was leaning: "If you're quite through with all that sentimental goo you've been dishing out, would you please stop blocking our doorway? Me and my boy have places to go and things to do before the sun drives us back underground."

I was so startled that I leapt to my feet and, when I did, the boulder pivoted with a coarse grinding sound to reveal an opening little more than three feet high. Half-fearing to behold a small troll crawling out of the exposed tunnel, I was quickly reassured by the upright emergence of two dwarves, a full-grown male and a much smaller one that I took to be a child. They were clothed alike in belted tunics, trousers, and hooded capes; on their feet they wore stout leather boots. Each of them carried a bundle that clanked metallically when they walked.

"Thankee kindly, miss. Hope old Darse didn't frighten you too much, but me and my boy, young Urka here, are on our way to the nearest Duodda encampment to trade some metalware for elven goods . . . and we've got to be back here before the sun comes up. How would I ever explain to the lad's mother that I let him be blinded on his very first trading trek?"

"That would indeed be a tragic turn of events, friend Darse, and we will delay you no longer," declared Formindar. "Go with the good will of Formindar and Aelas of the Muorra. And you can be sure your doorway will not be blocked again when you return to your tunnel before sunrise."

"'Tis a kindly thought, good elves; now sleep you well. Come along, Urka; bow your farewells and let's be on our way." Bending himself nearly in half, little Urka's bow was so cute that it was all I could do to suppress a giggle . . . but to do so would have hurt his feelings and offended his proud father, so I was glad I succeeded.

The two dwarves hurried off into the night. Formindar and I discussed this strange encounter—and dwarf lore generally—for a time before settling down to sleep.

We were wakened abruptly in the grey light of dawn by a blood-curdling scream of fear and rage. Leaping to our feet and looking for the source of the clamor, we quickly espied the dwarf Darse not fifty yards away, jumping up and down and shaking his fist skyward. There, beating its mighty wings laboriously, a great king-eagle was mounting slowly but steadily aloft, bearing its struggling prey—which was none other than young Urka, bleating like a pinioned hare! The young dwarf was fortunate that the eagle's talons had fastened in the bundle of trade furs strapped to Urka's back rather than into his living flesh . . . but once the eagle reached its aerie, the little lad's fate would be sealed in any event.

"Quick, Aelas, run as you have never run before and get directly beneath them!" No sooner had my uncle uttered those words than off I sped, soon darting past Darse and tracking the eagle's flight path as he slowly circled higher. I didn't see what happened next, but Formindar must have cast a powerful runic spell that stunned the eagle, for abruptly its talons lost their grip and, as the bird reeled drunkenly toward its mountain home, the precious cargo it had been carrying came plummeting earthward like a stone! Would I be able to close the distance in time to catch Urka before he crashed into the ground? I was anything but sure I could do it but, as they say, "fear lends wings to willing feet." I just could not bear to picture that cute little fellow's mangled body lying at my feet, so at the very last instant I was able to lunge far enough to make the catch. At that, the impact nearly tore Urka from my grasp. Somehow I managed to hang on and then gather Urka close against me so I could cushion his body when, staggering, I lost my balance altogether and slammed painfully into the ground with my right shoulder.

I barely had time to catch my breath and struggle into a sitting position—still clutching the sobbing Urka—before Darse was at my side, placing a gentle hand on my left shoulder and asking: "Are you alright, miss? And my boy . . . how is my boy?"

Between sobs Urka replied: "I'm not hurt, papa . . . just scared. That bad bird tried to carry me away, an' then he dropped me. That was the worst part! I thought sure I was a goner, but then that nice lady come runnin' ever so fast an' caught me just in the nick o' time."

"She did, my boy, she did, indeed," Darse said as he tousled Urka's hair. "Miss, I can't tell you how grateful I am to you, and to your uncle—for I know he magicked the eagle into dropping Urka. But I still can't believe what you did. When you took off running I was so certain you couldn't get there in time that I covered my eyes. I just couldn't bear to see him hit the ground. Then when I peeked between my fingers, I saw you flying through the air . . . reaching, arms full out, for my son. And you snatched him right out of the jaws of death as it were, for here he is . . . alive, thanks to you."

Darse, a tear trickling down each cheek, gently freed Urka from my protective grasp and felt him all over to be sure he had no broken bones. Uncle Formindar, who had arrived on the scene close behind Darse, told the dwarf that he was a healer and offered to check Urka as well, a favor Darse was quick to accept.

"Sound as a well-strung harp, I'd say, and none the worse for the adventure . . . which I'm sure he'll be telling family and friends about when he gets back to Svartalfheim. Which reminds me: in all the excitement, we've come perilously close to sunrise, so we need to get Urka—and you, of course—back underground right away, or Aelas' gallant rescue will go for naught."

We three adults scurried for the boulder pile, Darse carrying his son in his arms. It was fortunate that we hurried, for the gateway rock had scarcely been pivoted open and the dwarves safely into the tunnel when the sun peeked over the crest of the mountain to illuminate the plateau on which we stood.

Formindar was about to close the gateway from the outside, when Darse called out: "There's more I'd say to you now that Urka and I are safe from the sun's rays. So if you'd come into the tunnel a little ways . . . ."

My uncle and I accepted the dwarf's invitation and crept in on our hands and knees beyond the point where direct sunlight could reach, but where we could still see once our eyes had adjusted to the dim light. There we sat down facing Darse and Urka.

"Merely saying 'thank you' could never be payment enough for what you two did for my boy and me, so I want to give you a gift . . . ," declared Darse, pulling a pouch from beneath his tunic and fumbling with its drawstrings.

Formindar raised a hand in protest. "One should not accept a reward for saving a life, my friend. It isn't fitting."

"This isn't a reward; I've already told you it's a gift. There's a wise old saying that 'a gift calls for a gift'—it's a way to help keep the one who receives the first gift from feeling forever obligated to the giver, which can be a pretty heavy burden to bear. By saving Urka's life, you gave me back my dearest treasure, so to my way of thinking I want to gift you with my second greatest treasure . . . which you'll do me the honor of accepting if you don't wish to insult me and hurt my feelings."

"My apologies, good Darse . . . I can see that you are right. Aelas and I will, of course, be honored and deeply grateful to receive your gift."

"That's better," muttered the dwarf, apparently appeased. He dumped the contents of his neck pouch into one hand, and Formindar and I leaned forward to see what he was holding. It appeared to be a three-pointed stone and, as Darse turned it over in his palm, we could see that one side was white and the other red. A narrow gold band encircled the edge of the stone, separating the two sides. From the band a slender gold chain hung down, supporting what appeared to be a tiny iron Thor's hammer.

"Why," exclaimed Formindar, "that looks like a thunderstone! I've heard rumors that such powerful amulets existed, but I never expected to see one."

"Your knowledge of such arcane matters does you honor, Formindar. It is, indeed, a thunderstone . . . and here is how it works. If you strike the white surface lightly with the hammer, it will cause a violent hail storm; strike the red surface, and fire will erupt in a shower of sparks; and, finally, if you strike the gold band itself, enough sunshine will come forth to melt both snow and ice. Needless to say, no dwarf in his right mind would ever strike the gold band!" Placing the thunderstone back in its pouch, he handed it to my uncle.

"Take it with my thanks and blessings. Use it wisely, and only when your need is greatest. If you ever decide to visit Svartalfheim— and I hope that you will—just let any dwarves you meet know that Darse the Trader has named you dwarf-friend, and you'll be welcome throughout the realm." As he and Urka began their trek back down through the tunnel, Darse paused for a moment and added: "Oh, and when you go back to the Upper World, please close the door behind you."

And so—with smiles on our faces—we did!

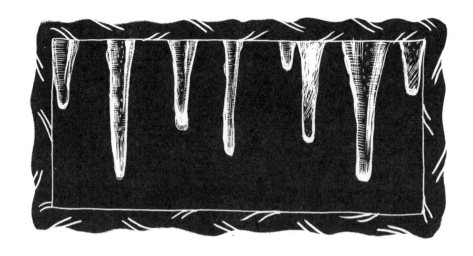

Heart of Ice

Prologue

Among the Light Elves, there is a much-beloved tale that goes something like this: There once was a beautiful elf-maid named Fawro, who was the pride of her tribe—the Duodda—and deeply loved by Oavar, one of the bravest of the elves. Hunting together in the birch forests, swimming in the mountain lakes, and telling stories beneath the starry sky, Fawro and Oavar took great joy in each other's company.

Alas, their joy was to be short-lived. One day while Fawro was swimming alone in the shallows of one of the lakes, Hjaki—a Frost Giant—spied her as he soared high overhead in his guise as an ice-eagle. Hjaki's frozen heart was melted by Fawro's loveliness, and he decided to have her as his bride. With Hjaki, to think was to act, so he immediately swooped down upon the unsuspecting elf-maid and snatched her up in his frosty talons. Fawro's terrified screams brought Oavar rushing to the lakeshore just in time to see the ice-eagle flying off into the eastern sky with Fawro dangling beneath him.

Hjaki brought Fawro to his home, a glittering palace of ice atop a rocky headland jutting out into a sullen, berg-filled sea. He gave her fine furs and rich food, and he tried to do everything he could to please her. Thus Hjaki could not understand why all she did was cry and insist that Oavar would come for her. Had she no appreciation for the cool, regal beauty of ice, and for the rugged good looks and awesome power of Hjaki? The answer clearly was "no" and, after a time, Hjaki's thawed heart began to freeze up again.

One morning, Fawro didn't come to breakfast, and Hjaki soon discovered that Oavar had, indeed, come during the night and stolen her away. The double set of elvish ski tracks leading toward the west were a silent testimony to what had taken place. Resuming the guise of an ice-eagle, Hjaki flew off in pursuit of the fugitives.

As soon as Hjaki alit in front of the two elves and transformed back into giant form, he cast an ice-rune on himself so that his body was protected by a flexible armor of ice. Oavar and Fawro loosed arrow after arrow against the giant, but none of the missiles could reach his flesh. Hjaki rushed at the couple, reaching them in just a few of his great strides. Seizing Fawro in one chilly hand and Oavar in the other, the Frost Giant cast yet another ice-rune on the elves, encasing each of them from head to toe in clear, glistening ice. Hjaki carried his living "statues" back to his ice palace by the sea, and, the last anyone heard, there they still stand—awaiting the thaw that will never come.

Or might it?

Aelas's Tale

After catching the dwarf-child, Urka, when the king-eagle dropped him from the sky, the shoulder I had fallen on proved to be more badly injured than I had first realized. With the excitement of our leave-taking from the two dwarves, I was able to ignore the discomfort for a time—especially if I avoided moving my right arm. Once Darse and Urka had departed for their home deep in the caverns of Svartalfheim, Uncle Formindar and I exited the dwarves' tunnel, closing and resealing the opening with the large boulder that served as its hidden door . . . and at the foot of which we had camped the night before.

It was while rolling up my sleeping fur preparatory to resuming our trek to the nearest Duodda encampment that my shoulder twinged painfully enough to cause me to wince and grimace. Ever one to react to the slightest change in a companion's posture or facial expression, my uncle cocked his head like a wise old owl and asked: "What is the matter, Aelas? Did you hurt your shoulder when you fell?"

"I hate to complain, but I'm afraid I may have done just that. It's not too painful if I don't move it, but if I do . . . well, it's pretty bad. Could you take a look at my shoulder and see if I might have broken something?"

When Formindar nodded in agreement, I unbelted my tunic and—turning my back toward him—pulled my shirt up over my head to fully expose my shoulder for his examination. Even such a simple act as that brought excruciating pain, requiring as it did far more stretching and arm rotation than my poor shoulder could tolerate . . . and I grunted audibly.

"Poor girl! I'm afraid your heroic deed is costing you dearly. Well, let me check your shoulder and upper arm, and we'll see how bad the damage is."

My uncle ran his fingers over the injured area, gently squeezing here and probing there to determine the condition of the underlying bones, muscles, and sinews. Then, placing his left hand firmly atop my shoulder and grasping me by my elbow, he slowly moved my arm through its normal rotary motions . . . carefully watching my face to see which positions caused me to wince. When he was finished with the examination, Formindar helped me put my tunic back on . . . then rendered the verdict I was so anxiously awaiting.

"Good news! You should heal just fine over time . . . no bones are broken nor sinews torn loose. Your muscles did take quite a beating, so there is going to be a lot of bruising . . . and swelling, too, unless we can find a glacier-fed stream nearby and apply an ice-cold compress to the injured area. Once any swelling has subsided, you should gradually resume normal arm motions and activities—if nothing else, to be sure the area gets enough blood flow."

"Heal over time, you said, Uncle? Why can't you just use your runic powers to heal my shoulder right now?"

"My dear girl, have you forgotten all my warnings about not using magic except as a last resort? Were your life at risk—or if you would be permanently crippled without magical intervention—of course I would act. But each use of magic exacts its price from the wielder, and it would be foolish to diminish one's magical resources by healing someone whom nature would restore in due time.

"Mind you, I'm not saying that wizards have only a finite amount of magical power at their disposal . . . and that when it is used up, it is gone forever. But it is true that each time a wizard does expend magical energy, it drains his reserves—and usually weakens him physically as well. In that state he cannot perform any other acts of magic until he has rested and, through ritual and meditation, reconnected with the source of his powers. In my case, of course, that source is the Light."

Somewhat chagrined, but intrigued by the wizard lore that my uncle was revealing, I spoke up. "Now I see what you mean, or at least I think I do. If you were to heal my shoulder now, and some real emergency should happen later in the day—or however long the period is that you need to restore your powers—you probably wouldn't be able to deal with the situation magically, and that might prove disastrous for you or someone you were trying to help." When Formindar nodded, I continued. "Had I realized the situation more clearly, I would have curbed my impatience and not pestered you about using magic to heal me. I hope you'll forgive me."

My uncle smiled as he replied: "I think we have both learned from this experience. I need to remember that curious minds such as yours and Dag's deserve fuller explanations than mere admonitory declarations. So I apologize to you also, my dear, and I promise to be more respectful of your intelligence in the future."

He continued: "As for your lesson, Aelas, I hope you now realize that accepting the realities of life—rather than futilely insisting they be altered to suit our desires—is a large step along the path to attaining *lotkulas*, a goal for which every Light Elf strives." Formindar chuckled: "But enough philosophizing! Let us find that glacial stream and see about relieving the swelling in your shoulder."

Fortunately, we hadn't traveled more than half a mile or so before we found just the kind of stream my uncle had been looking for. In no time at all, he had removed his spare tunic from his backpack, soaked it in the icy water, and—after wringing it out—wrapped it securely around my injured shoulder and upper arm. While we waited for the cold compress to have an effect, he took a pinch of shredded willow bark from his medicine bag and instructed me to chew it up thoroughly, then swallow it. It had a bitter taste that made me wrinkle my face in a grimace, but Formindar assured me that the awful-tasting stuff should help to ease the pain in my shoulder. Obviously he knew far more about the art of healing than I did, so I didn't argue.

It was apparent to both of us that I would be unable to use a bow effectively for quite some time to come, and this posed something of a dilemma. To depend for meat on what Raiko and Darra could kill—and we could supplement by setting snares—would likely result in all four of us having to survive on pretty short rations for a time. Thus it seemed we had the choice of either returning to the forests of Vuobmai as directly and quickly as possible, or seeking out the nearest Duodda encampment and availing ourselves of their hospitality. Because the latter option promised to be much nearer at hand, we chose it—despite the emotional appeal of going home to heal in the security of our family.

Darra didn't seem to care so long as she could stay by my side, licking my hand in sympathy. As for Raiko, I doubt if he gave the matter a second's thought—wherever my uncle went, the goshawk intended to go with him.

Once we resumed walking, it was a matter of only a few hours before we came upon a large encampment of elven tents, probably the same one Darse and Urka had visited the night before. Unlike in our forest village, the tents of the Duodda sat on no permanent sites but were made to be moved whenever the band chose to change locations in pursuit of the migratory herds of wild reindeer. The relatively few reindeer the Duodda had tamed in order to have a reliable source of milk and cheese also served as draft animals to drag the long tent poles along and carry the bulkier packs on their backs when the Duodda joined the annual migration. At that time, a few of the band's reindeer even pulled small, boat-shaped sleds to transport the very young—and very old—elves who might otherwise have had a hard time keeping up with the others.

Be that as it may, the dogs in the encampment soon let the Duodda know that they had company, and before long it seemed that every tent must have disgorged its residents—laughing and chattering like a flock of magpies—to see and greet the new visitors. How unlike they were from the more restrained and sedate elves of my forest home. Could it possibly be that living one's life beneath the open sky makes that much difference in the personality of a whole tribe?

I was also struck immediately by how much taller the Duodda

seemed to be than any of the Muorra or Merin I knew. Not as tall as humans, of course, but certainly overtopping other elves by several inches. It almost seemed as if their bodies had elongated in these open spaces—as had the bows they carried. Could this be part of an emerging pattern? Hmm . . . I would have to keep my eyes and ears open during our visit among the Duodda and ponder this matter further.

This was not the time for reflection, however, for several of our new friends linked arms with us—avoiding my right arm after Formindar hastily cautioned them—and noisily escorted us to the tent of their head-woman, Muöre. It seemed as if the whole band was about to follow us in, but Muöre—with just a few choice words— shooed away all but a few of her closest advisors.

"Dear me," she exclaimed in a tone of bemused exasperation, "at times like this my band acts just like a group of children with a new toy! You should have seen them last night when we were visited by a dwarf trader and his son. You would have thought my people had never seen dwarves before, which of course they have. They pestered those little folk so long that I finally had to put a stop to it so the poor trader could conduct his business and the two of them could get back underground before the sun came up. I do hope they made it."

Uncle Formindar assured Muöre that the dwarves had done just that. Then he proceeded to recount our adventure with them, concluding with a description of my injury and a request for Duodda hospitality until I healed enough to use my bow comfortably and proficiently—thus being able to contribute fully to the safety and well-being of the two of us and our animal companions.

"You and your niece are welcome to stay in my village as long as you like, Guardian," Muöre stated. "I would offer to put my skills as a healer at her disposal, but I am sure that I could do no more for her than you have already done—and undoubtedly intend to continue doing." Turning to the advisor on her left, the head-woman directed him: "Bissovas, please have someone set up one of the spare tents as soon as possible for our guests so they can enjoy some privacy when they feel the need for it."

Bissovas arose at once and slipped out of the tent to see that the task was done. Muöre nodded in satisfaction as she turned her attention back to Formindar.

"Your unexpected arrival is most timely. There is a matter that I feel calls for the Guardian's attention, and I was about to send you a message requesting a visit. However, we will discuss that another day when we can be joined by the principal elders of the other Duodda bands. It should take no more than a week for the farthest of them to come here, and I am sure it will take Aelas longer than that to heal fully."

My uncle nodded agreement. "It must be a serious matter, indeed, if you feel the need to call for a full conclave."

"Oh, it is . . . as I am sure you will agree when you hear what it is. But I do not wish to speak more of it until the others are here to listen—and to take part in the discussion, as well. You are just going to have to call on some of that patience for which you are so famous."

I could have sworn that a slight smile curled Muöre's lips as she spoke, but whether she was laughing with Formindar—or at him— was not clear to me . . . and I found that more than a little unsettling.

Muöre's voice seemed to harden as she resumed: "Meanwhile, Guardian, there is a personal question to which I would very much like an answer. Why have you kept my grandson away from me? My sources tell me that it has been three winters since Völund's son first entered Alfheim, yet never once has he visited his father's people— the Duodda. This is a serious breach of courtesy, Guardian, and I must insist on an explanation!" The head-woman was extremely agitated now, and her voice retained only the thinnest veneer of politeness.

I was stunned to learn that this stern old elf-woman was Dag's grandmother, and that she held my uncle responsible for Dag's failure to pay her a courtesy call. Small wonder I had been feeling increasingly uneasy in her presence! That such a tough-minded person could emerge from among the fun-loving Duodda also came as a surprise.

Formindar, however, seemed to ignore Muöre's accusatory tone as he calmly responded: "Did your sources also tell you that Dag only spent one year in my village? Odin sent the young man to Alfheim to learn the Alfar Way by living in a community of Light Elves and being mentored by a lore-wise elder. Whether it was the All-Father's intention that Dag come to me, or our paths were brought together by the Light, I cannot say. I only know that when we first met he risked his life to save mine, then grieved with me over the death of my slain dog-companion as if it had been his own. I was drawn to him as I have been drawn to no other, and we became sworn-brothers— living in the same tent, sharing the same meals. Our days were filled with exploration, lore, and life-lessons learned. Dag was such a quick learner and showed so much integrity that I soon came to respect him deeply and trust him completely . . . so much so that I asked him to partner with my niece, Aelas, in the Great Hunt. He readily agreed, and their successful Hunt culminated in the ritual by which they became fang-mates.

"I had every intention of bringing Dag here to meet you—and Aelas, too—once the excitement had abated. Alas, for my plan, Odin had others. The very next day the All-Father sent one of his ravens to our village to bid Dag leave Alfheim at once—and alone—to resume the role of an itinerant storyteller. This he has done, and we have seen neither hide nor hair of him for the past two winters, which grieves Aelas and me deeply.

"I am revealing to you so much that is personal, private, and painful. I do this both so will know what has become of your grandson, and so you will understand that I did not deliberately keep him from you while he was in my charge. I had no idea that Odin was going to exile Dag from Alfheim at all—let alone so abruptly— thus I could not have anticipated that the need to bring Dag to you would prove so urgent. I can well understand your disappointment and frustration. I sincerely apologize for my mistake in judgment, but I hope you will accept that this is all that it was—a mistake, not an intentional slight or insult."

Muöre sniffed audibly: "I suppose I will have to do so since your explanation sounds so plausible . . . but I would have expected the judgment of our Guardian to be less fallible."

"So would I, Muöre, so would I," Formindar responded gently, "but being chosen for the post does not endow the new Guardian with godlike wisdom. No, the wisdom to carry out my responsibilities is something for which I must strive every day of my life, and that—more often than not—means learning from my mistakes. Being able to quaff a horn of wisdom from the giant Mimir's Well—as did Odin—is not an opportunity given to an elf. I am sorry to have disappointed you, and I will try not to do so too often in the future . . . but I can make no promises."

Muöre hmmphed, but she chose not to press the issue further. The atmosphere remained tense, however, and I'm sure that my uncle was as relieved as I was—and probably Muöre as well—when Bissovas reappeared to inform us that our tent was ready. Taking our leave of the head-woman, we followed Bissovas to the only place of relative privacy we were to enjoy for the ensuing week.

As soon as we were by ourselves, I began to blurt out my resentment at the way Muöre had treated Formindar. He quickly hushed my protests with a reminder that in a tent "the walls might have ears," and private matters were better spoken about the next time we could be alone on the open fjell where no one could approach us unobserved.

<hr />

The week passed fairly quickly. Despite Muöre's aloofness, the other members of her band seemed eager to spend time with us. They insisted we share their meals, which were always a time for gossip and questions and tale-telling. The Duodda were very curious about our adventures, and they were eager to show us the things that were important to them. The younger women delighted in displaying their children—whom I made a point to praise as extravagantly as honesty permitted—and the younger men were only too happy to demonstrate the long bows (as tall as they were) that permitted them to send an arrow much farther than could one of my tribe's shorter, recurved bows. Proud as they were of their own gear, however, the archers expressed so much curiosity about my Muorra bow that I truly regretted not being sound enough of limb to demonstrate it for them.

We also compared knives, and I don't know if they were any more curious about my fairly short-bladed one of dragon bone than I was about the long, slender dwarvish blades of steel they had acquired by trade from their underground neighbors.

Except for small details of decoration, our clothing was much alike. But there was one other distinctive feature that set the members of our two tribes apart: no Muorra wore their hair extending below the shoulder, whereas the hair of every Duodda I'd seen reached down at least to the middle of the back! Each female wore hers up in whatever arrangement suited the individual, presumably to keep her hair out of the stew pot or otherwise interfere with some other activity in which she was engaged. The males gathered their hair at the back of the head, secured it there with a leather thong, and let the rest hang down like a horse's tail. It was a style that undoubtedly worked well on the open fjell . . . but in the forests of Vuobmai it would have proven disastrous. The first thicket one of these fine-looking fellows tried to push through would have snagged him by his magnificent mane as quickly as one of my uncle's snares would entangle a snow grouse. Small wonder we Muorra wear our hair short!

Small groups of elders from the other Duodda bands had been drifting into the encampment for several days, and at last Muöre declared the council could begin. Formindar, greeting each party as it arrived, had discreetly attempted to determine the object of the gathering, but each of the elders professed to be as puzzled as he.

There was a buzz of excitement in the air when the sacred fire was lit and dedicated to the Light—of which the fire was one manifestation. The council site thus sanctified, Muöre stepped forward to address the assembled elders.

"As you know, my kinsmen, I would not have summoned you to a grand council save for the most pressing of matters—something of the gravest concern to us all." Satisfied that she had the full attention of the assembled elves, Muöre pressed on. "You are all familiar with the fate of Fawro and Oavar of the Twin Lakes Band. How she was stolen away by that wicked Frost Giant, Hjaki, and when Oavar sought to rescue her from Hjaki's ice palace in uttermost Jötunheim, the giant magicked them both into living statues of ice. So said the rumors that drifted back to us, and so the truth of it was confirmed by the gyrfalcons that were sent out to serve as our eyes . . . and which have continued to report over the years that the statues still stand in Hjaki's palace."

Turning to Formindar, Muöre asked: "Why has this situation been permitted to continue, Guardian?" She spat out that honorable title as if it left a bad taste in her mouth. "Why have those poor young elves been forced to remain in their frozen bondage for all these years? We would have sent a band of elvish warriors to rescue them long ago had the Guardian before you not stayed our hands. 'For the peace and safety of all Alfheim,' he said. Rank cowardice I called it then . . . and I declare it again today.

"And when he chose you to become Guardian after him, Formindar of the Muorra, you continued to follow his weak-kneed example in this matter. How could the Frost Giants possibly fail to be convinced that they can raid Alfheim with impunity?"

Muöre's voice had risen steadily higher with each declaration and she was almost shouting as she queried shrilly: "Well, Guardian, what have you to say for yourself?"

The council members were stirring uncomfortably, upset by Muöre's rudeness toward a guest in her village, by recognition that the concerns she had raised were shared by many of the Duodda, and by the growing realization that the outcome of this confrontation might well shatter their peaceful lives for the foreseeable future. A sea of anxious eyes and ears were fixed on Formindar as he slowly rose to his feet and, drawing his quiet dignity about him like a cloak, responded to the head-woman's verbal attack.

"I hear your concerns, Muöre, and I know they come from your heart. What elf could possibly think about the twin fates of Fawro and Oavar without being filled with pity for them . . . or anger at their captor, the Frost Giant Hjaki? And what elf does not feel threatened by—and resentful of—the violation of Alfheim itself, our sacred homeland?"

The audience nodded in agreement as Formindar continued: "Yet having acknowledged these very real and natural feelings, we must also remember that fear and anger are the enemies of *lotkulas*, which lies at the very heart of the Alfar Way and must always shape the actions of our people. It was this principle that governed my predecessor's decision not to sanction sending a war band deep into Jötunheim to rescue Fawro and Oavar, and to punish Hjaki. I supported his decision then, again when I became the Guardian of Alfheim, and I support it today.

"Let me remind you of the reasons for this decision. What Hjaki did in abducting Fawro was clearly wrong by elvish standards, but 'bride-capture' is not an uncommon custom in some other societies— especially among the giants. If the tale that has come down to us is true in all its details, apparently that is what Hjaki thought he was doing . . . carrying off his bride-to-be. Fawro obviously did not look at what had happened in this light—nor did Oavar—but it is an important point to remember, nevertheless. Oavar thought he was rescuing his beloved from her wicked abductor; Hjaki saw Oavar as a stranger who had invaded his home to carry off his bride. Whose perspective was right? Elves and giants would be bound to disagree on this point, yet it is critical to understanding what happened next.

"When Hjaki realized that his 'bride' had been stolen from him, he understandably pursued Fawro and Oavar to bring her back. Not wanting to go back, the elves—also understandably—resisted and, in doing so, used deadly force against a much larger and stronger foe. It was at that point—and only at that point—when Hjaki lost his self-control and used deadly force in return, casting an ice rune that permanently encased Fawro and Oavar in blocks of ice.

"To us that was a wicked act; to the Frost Giants it would seem a natural consequence of the elves' behavior. My predecessor as Guardian concluded that any war band attempting to rescue Fawro and Oavar would likely meet the same fate. But, even if they were successful, their act surely would be seen by the other Frost Giants as an invasion from Alfheim, thus inviting massive retaliation . . . and an elf-giant war could devastate all we hold dear. That there have been no giant incursions since Hjaki's all those years ago should put to rest Muöre's notion that the Frost Giants consider the Light Elves too weak or cowardly to defend their own. No, it seems more reasonable to conclude that the giants either have no great desire to violate Alfheim's borders, or they are no more eager to provoke a major conflict than we should be."

The head-nodding and mutters of approval that flowed throughout the council clearly infuriated Muöre, who leapt to her feet, shook a forefinger at my uncle, and shouted: "Are you all so eager for peace at any price that you are willing to overlook what is going on here? Well, I am not. The facts remain that an elf-maid was stolen from within Alfheim by a Frost-Giant, and that she and her would-be rescuer are being held against their wills. This situation clearly calls for action by the Guardian, who is refusing to do anything and will not permit the rest of us to act, either. There is an ancient provision in the Alfar Way that a Guardian who fails to carry out his responsibilities can be Challenged. Very well. I, Muöre, acting in accordance with our ancient customs, hereby offer a formal Challenge to Formindar in the presence of this council of the Duodda: either bring about the return of Fawro and Oavar, or step down as Guardian and let someone else be appointed in your stead—someone who is not afraid to do what is right!"

I was stunned by this turn of events as were, it seemed, most of the council. But apparently my unflappable uncle was unconcerned. He raised one hand—palm outstretched—to calm the buzz of excited voices before responding to the head-woman's declaration.

"Some might question if this is a proper forum for such a Challenge inasmuch as the other two tribes who are served by the Guardian are not present." Several nodding heads among the council revealed that this point had already crossed their minds. "Still, since the victims are members of this tribe alone, I will not make an issue of the Challenge's legality. I must say, however, that I continue to have serious reservations about the wisdom of mounting an expedition. But, since a formal Challenge has been issued, I will accept it personally rather than abdicate my responsibilities as Guardian and risk having a less cautious successor put the very survival of Alfheim at risk. One thing more will I say: because this quest will be rife with uncertainty and extreme peril, I refuse to endanger the lives of any other elves—I will seek out Hjaki's ice palace by myself!"

This declaration was followed by a multitude of gasps, then a stunned silence that was soon interrupted by my anguished and vigorous protest: "Oh, no, Uncle Formindar, you're not going into that Frost Giant's lair all by yourself . . . I'm going with you! We've experienced many a hardship in the past and we've always overcome them. I understand the dangers involved in this quest, but I'm willing to face them, too . . . if we can do it together—along with Darra and Raiko, of course. Just give me time enough to get my shoulder fully healed, and I'll be ready to go."

My uncle embraced me in one of his warm hugs. Then, holding me at arm's length, he declared: "Bless your brave and generous heart, my dear. We'll leave for home tomorrow to complete your healing. Then, if your parents have no objections, of course you may go with me. After all, we are a team, are we not?"

During the rest of that day—and even the next morning up until the moment of our departure—Formindar and I were besieged by

Duodda wishing us well, giving us advice, and some even offering to join our quest. We thanked them one-and-all for their kindness, but my uncle remained adamant against risking any more lives than our own, or taking a chance of provoking a wider conflict with the Frost Giants. As we departed we felt embraced and uplifted by the warm goodwill of all the Duodda—all save one, that is. Muöre, head-woman though she was, did not turn out to see us off . . . nor did she send a message wishing us well on our quest—one which she had initiated! Much as I wanted to think well of Dag's grandmother for his sake, I couldn't help but wonder "what kind of viper was gnawing her innards" to make her so spiteful. I silently vowed to ask Formindar later if he knew.

Our return trip to our home village in the forests of Vuobmai was uneventful, as were the following months of healing and restrengthening my shoulder, and the subsequent retraining of my archery skills under the watchful eye of my father, Skuttar. Where we planned to go, we could not afford to have me in anything less than my top condition. By the time the leaves began to acquire their fall colors, I could assure my uncle that I was as good as new and eager to accompany him to Jötunheim.

The shortest path to Jötunheim led us once again through the territory of the Duodda but not by way of Muöre's village, which I was quite content to by-pass. My uncle could see nothing to be gained by another encounter with Dag's grandmother, a sentiment I shared completely. When Formindar and I had discussed her attitude during our earlier journey back to Vuobmai, he revealed that just prior to his selection as Guardian, it was no secret among the elders of Alfheim that Muöre wanted the position . . . and fully expected to be chosen. When she was passed over—to her thinking—in favor of Formindar, she felt both humiliated and infuriated. Modest and unassuming as he is, my uncle had not sought to be named Guardian (which may even have been one of the reasons he was chosen!), yet Muöre seemed to hold Formindar personally responsible for thwarting her ambition. Even putting aside—as best I was able—my own bias in favor of my uncle, I could only be thankful that Muöre had not been selected to be the Guardian of Alfheim. Her attitudes and actions seemed to be badly out-of-step with the Alfar Way!

We did stop overnight at Boatka, the principal village of the Twin Lakes Band of the Duodda. Situated as the encampment was near the foot of the mountain-ringed plateau that formed the adjoining part of Jötunheim, Boatka marked the last outpost of elvish civilization in this part of Alfheim. Once we crossed the unmarked border between the two realms, my uncle and I would be moving—with each step we took—farther and farther away from the lands we knew and loved, and into the frozen wastes that were the home of the Frost Giants.

Fortunately, before we had left Muöre's village earlier in the year, Formindar had talked at length with the visiting delegation from the Twin Lakes Band, and he had convinced them that it was only fair that they outfit us on our quest to recover their missing young people. And outfit us they did that last morning, providing warm outerwear, thick sleeping furs, dried foods, and a boat-shaped sled to carry them—complete with a tame reindeer to pull the load. They also insisted we leave our shorter, broader forestland skis with them for safekeeping, and take, instead, the longer, narrower Duodda skis, which were more suitable for travel in open country. Their generosity was heart-warming and, nearly overwhelmed with gratefulness, we pledged to do everything in our power to reunite them with their loved ones.

On that note we took our departure from Boatka, accompanied only by one of the hunters who agreed to guide us to the pass leading from Alfheim into Jötunheim—a pass guarded at all times so that the villagers could be alerted should the Frost Giants choose to launch a surprise attack. None had happened in recent memory, but Hjaki's abduction of Fawro had been enough to reinforce long-standing fears and insure that the pass guards took their responsibility seriously.

Winter had come early to Jötunheim, and enough snow had

drifted down the pass that we and our guide—one Jallo by name—did not have to struggle for long helping the reindeer pull the sled. Soon its runners found a smoother traction on the accumulating snow, and the upward climb became much easier. Jallo stayed with us until we reached the guard post, a sturdy lean-to partially sheltered by a rock ledge but commanding a clear view of the upper portion of the pass. No one should be able to slip past here unseen—especially anyone as large as a Frost Giant!

Seated in the lean-to, wrapped in a fur robe and warming his hands over a small fire, was the current pass watcher, an elf named Duostel to whom Jallo introduced us. We all gossiped for a few minutes, then Jallo and Duostel traded places. Jallo took up his turn at being the pass watcher while Duostel headed back down the pass to his tent in Boatka and to a well-earned rest. Bidding them both farewell, my uncle and I turned our feet up the pass where at some point we passed beyond the ken of elvenkind and entered into Jötunheim to face the unknown perils posed by the world of the Frost Giants.

Of the ensuing days before we came at last in sight of Hjaki's ice-clad abode, there is little enough I care to say . . . and not much that I choose to remember. At that time of the year, the chariot of the Sun barely rises above the horizon—and then only briefly—so our trek seemed to me to take place during a nearly endless period of semi-darkness and unrelenting, bone-chilling, finger-numbing cold. Save for the generosity of the Twin Lakes Band in providing us with such excellent winter clothing—not to mention the food supplies and a way to transport them—I seriously doubt we would have survived the trip. I'm certain I would not have done so.

As it was, more than once I was so cold and exhausted I was ready to give up and fall—relieved—into the welcoming arms of a glistening snow bank, beckoning me with its tantalizing visions of warmth and rest. But had I given in to its false promises I would have slipped into the sleep that never ends, and my poor uncle would have been left to carry on the quest without me. I could not bear to abandon him that way and add to his other burdens, so each time I was tempted I was able to find the inner strength to resist and endure.

The day (or was it night?) came at long last when our eyes were drawn to a light gleaming on the horizon, too low to be a bright star and too fixed to be the Northern Lights.

"At last!" exclaimed Formindar. "That has to be Hjaki's ice palace. It is no illusion, and there are no other dwellings reputed to be in this part of Jötunheim. For that matter, who but Frost Giants could live in a place like this?"

"If you're trying to raise my spirits, Uncle Formindar, what you just said isn't helping much. What do we do now that we're almost there?"

"I have been pondering that question ever since I agreed to undertake this quest in the first place. Since I want to avoid violence if at all possible, it seems we have only two options. Either we sneak into the palace, disenchant Fawro and Oavar, and the four of us sneak back out and trek back to Alfheim—all the while avoiding detection and pursuit by Hjaki and his servants—or . . . ."

"Or what, Uncle?"

"Or we go openly to Hjaki's palace portal, request an audience, and see if we can convince him to release his captives. That choice, if successful, would avoid all the skulking about, not to mention the threat of pursuit and the violent confrontation sure to follow—a confrontation we would be hard pressed to survive."

"And if we aren't successful in convincing him?" I asked apprehensively.

Formindar shrugged his shoulders and gave me a wry smile. "Well, then I imagine we are apt to have that violent confrontation a bit sooner. Still, I believe I would rather risk talking with Hjaki than not. Who knows, perhaps after all this time he has even come to regret what he did and will welcome an opportunity to make amends?"

I'm not sure my uncle truly believed this outcome to be a strong likelihood any more than I did, but I did not challenge his choice. It was far more in keeping with his character—as I knew it—than either skulking about or violence would ever be, and that was good enough for me. As it turned out, the final outcome of our quest proved to be far stranger than anything either of us could have anticipated.

Once we had drawn almost, but not quite, close enough to Hjaki's abode to be seen, we pulled the sled in behind a large outcrop of snow-covered rocks where we cached it for future need. We fed and tethered the reindeer there and, after feeding our dog and goshawk companions, gave Darra and Raiko verbal and visual instructions to stay near the cache and guard it as best they could. Darra whined and Raiko flapped his wings in frustration, but both of them obeyed.

Turning our skis once more toward the ice palace, we soon arrived at its tall doorway, which was carved from a single huge block of ice. It looked to be immovable, but when Formindar called out our names and requested an audience with "Lord Hjaki," the great door swung silently open and the giant gatekeeper bade us enter. The gatekeeper must have been convinced we were something more than a pair of elvish vagabonds, for he ushered us into a small waiting room where he told us to divest ourselves of our skis and my bow while he went off to announce our presence to Hjaki. I foresaw an interminable wait ahead of us, but much to my surprise, the gatekeeper soon returned to inform us that "Lord Hjaki has graciously consented" to see us at once. Either Hjaki was so starved for news from the outside world that he would have welcomed any stranger who wandered by or, just perhaps, Formindar's name could gain entry in places far beyond the boundaries of Alfheim. The answer to that question was soon provided by Hjaki himself.

We were ushered into the main hall of the palace and our presence announced. Sitting atop a massive throne on an elevated dais at the far end of the room was Hjaki—Lord by title, but kingly in all his trappings.

"Come forward, elves, come forward," Hjaki's voice boomed. "I won't bite. Haw, haw, haw."

So forward we went, one step at a time. Curious as I was about seeing a Frost Giant face-to-face, I could not help glancing from side to side to take in the hall itself. I couldn't tell if any other building materials had been used in constructing Hjaki's palace, but everything that met my eyes was made entirely of ice—the floor, the walls, the ceiling . . . even the tables and chairs and, of course, the throne. Standing to one side of the dais were the objects of our quest, the icy blocks encasing Fawro and Oavar.

By then we had reached the open area in front of the throne, and our full attention was drawn to the figure of Hjaki. And an imposing figure he was. Even seated he towered over us; later, when I saw him on his feet, I figured he must have stood more than fifteen feet tall. And he wasn't just tall, he was also big-boned and meaty beneath his hooded robes of ice-bear skins. Hjaki's visage was rugged and, as befit a Frost Giant, his craggy eyebrows were coated with hoarfrost while icicles encased his sparse but long chin hairs. His glacial blue eyes fixed each of us as he spoke.

"Formindar of the Muorra, eh? I've heard of you." Hjaki nodded thoughtfully to himself. "So then, what brings the Guardian of Alfheim so far from his homeland . . . and into mine? I am not one of your charges." The giant's voice had grown more menacing.

"No, you are not, but I have come at the behest of those who are my charges to plead for the return of two young elves whom you imprisoned many years ago and have held ever since. Their families are anxious to welcome them home."

"Ah, yes," growled Hjaki, "I do seem to remember those elves you're asking about. The maid was supposed to be my bride, and the other one tried to steal her away from me. She was just as bad as he was—when he came for her, she willingly ran off with him. And, when I went after them to bring her back, they even tried to kill me!

After that I would have been justified in slaying both of them, but I decided to be merciful. I froze them both and have kept their 'statues' here in my hall as a reminder not to be so foolish as to fall in love again. That elf-maid's beauty had thawed my frozen heart, but after she rejected all I had to offer her, it iced over once more. I vowed then and there my heart would never again be touched by anything but ice . . . and it never has been!

"Still, I must admit those 'statues' also stand as a constant reminder that the elf-maid didn't want to marry me—and that is not an easy thing to live with. So I might be willing to have you take them off my hands, if . . . ."

"If what, Lord Hjaki?" queried Formindar eagerly.

"If you will provide me with another bride in exchange for the first one. And I'll toss the male into the bargain, free and clear. You can't ask for fairer than that now, can you?"

My uncle seemed momentarily befuddled. "But . . . but I thought you just said you never intended to fall in love again. What use would you have for another bride?"

Hjaki chortled hilariously and slapped his knees. "Love? What's love got to do with it? I need a wife to warm my bed, give me strong sons, and—oh, yes—mend my socks."

"I understand what your requirements are, Lord Hjaki," Formindar responded far more diplomatically than I would have, "but I have no idea where I could find a woman who might choose to meet them."

"Oh, I don't think you'd need to look very far," said the giant, staring fixedly at me with an unsettling smile on his lips. "This comely niece of yours would suit me just fine. Yes, indeed, an elf-maid for an elf-maid seems like a fair exchange, does it not?"

I cast a panicked glance at my now shaken uncle, who blurted out: "No, no, that's not possible. You can't have her!"

His mask of affability cast aside, a glowering Hjaki rose to his feet and declared: "You say 'no' and 'can't' to *me*, elf? You forget where you are and who I am. Aelas *is* my choice, and I *will* have her . . . now!"

Stepping down from the dais and bending toward me, Hjaki grabbed me by one arm and swept me off my feet. When he hoisted me to the level of his face and puckered his lips, I screamed and tried to push away from him with my free arm. Averting my head from the giant's eager lips, I heard Formindar's anguished cry of "This must not be!" and saw him pull the dwarf's thunderstone from his pouch. Holding it aloft, my uncle struck the gold rim of the stone with the tiny Thor's hammer attached to it, declaring as he did so: "Bring forth the Light!"

And there was Light. It was as if the sun itself had risen right there in Hjaki's hall and brought with it instant Spring. Cracks appeared in the walls as the ice began a rapid melting, and soon pieces of the ceiling were falling all about us . . . one even coming down on Hjaki's head. Bellowing in rage as his beloved palace literally dissolved around him, the giant sought out the cause of his distress and loss—Formindar! My uncle tried to elude Hjaki, but he slipped in a puddle on the icy floor and fell. Before Formindar could rise, the giant's massive foot pinned him down where he lay.

"Now I'm going to kneel on you and crush you for the miserable, meddling bug that you are. Guard yourself if you can, Guardian."

I still dangled by one arm from Hjaki's hand, although he apparently had forgotten about me in his pursuit of my uncle. In desperation, I grasped one of the giant's ice-covered chin hairs and yanked it out at its roots. Despite the melting that was going on, I found myself holding onto a long needle of ice, which I jabbed deep into Hjaki's chest in the hope that the pain might distract his attention from Formindar.

Much to my surprise, the giant staggered several steps backward, fell to his knees, and—looking deeply into my eyes—asked, as if in amazement, "Why?" We stared thus at each other until the light in his pale blue eyes flickered out—and Hjaki was no more. I had killed this being, face-to-face, and I felt as if a part of my spirit had departed with his.

Uncle Formindar was sitting up now a short distance away, clearly still shaken by his close call. "It seems, perhaps, that Hjaki spoke more truly than he realized when he said his heart could only be touched by ice. Ice was his life . . . and also his death, poor fellow." My uncle sighed. "Well, Aelas, why don't you see what has become of Fawro and Oavar. I will join you in a moment."

I stumbled over to where the two "statues" lay, tumbled onto the floor by the collapse of Hjaki's melting palace . . . and thawing like everything else. As I knelt beside them and anxiously watched, the ice that had enclosed the two elves slowly disappeared. I don't know what I had been expecting at this point, but the shrunken gray visages of the fabled lovers were definitely not a promising sight!

Becoming aware of Formindar's presence standing close behind me, I grasped his hand and gasped: "Something is horribly wrong, Uncle. They aren't breathing at all, and they look just awful. Oh, please use your magic to heal them!"

Speaking not a word, Formindar knelt beside me and closely examined the bodies of Fawro and Oavar, even placing his long, sensitive fingers on their faces, chests, and wrists. Then, with even a deeper sigh than he had bestowed on Hjaki's fate, my uncle turned toward me to say: "At times I can heal the living, my dear—even one teetering on the brink between life and death, like Aratak's son, the dragonet Suonjar—but not even I can call back the dead. And the spirits of Fawro and Oavar departed from their bodies many years ago to be embraced by the Light."

"Dead? How could they be dead? If Dag could survive being frozen in ice, why couldn't they?"

Formindar looked me in the face, his eyes full of love and pity: "A perfectly fair question, Aelas. I only wish I could answer it with certainty . . . but I cannot. Runic spells are very tricky and unpredictable, and it seems that the intent of the spell-caster may have a powerful effect on the outcome. Dag's uncle froze him as an act of love to preserve his nephew from the dragon Nidhögg's venom . . . and so it did. Hjaki, on the other hand, froze Fawro and Oavar as an act of malice . . . and it killed them. 'Blame not the runes but the spirit of the caster' as the old saying goes."

"To have gone through all that we have only to find the lovers dead is almost too much to bear," I sobbed.

"Indeed," my uncle remarked as his comforting arms enfolded me, "it would seem that there are times when legends might better be allowed to remain legends."

Epilogue

Formindar runically refroze the bodies of Fawro and Oavar so that he and Aelas might safely transport them by sled to Boatka, where the parents of the deceased and the rest of the Twin Lakes Band could inter the remains properly within the sacred confines of Alfheim. Hjaki's servants had all fled from the collapse of the ice palace and made no effort to interfere with the return trek of Formindar and Aelas to Alfheim.

When Muöre learned about the outcome of the quest for Fawro and Oavar, she relinquished her position as the head-woman of her band. She retired to a small tent on the outskirts of her village, there to continue sharing her skills as a healer with her kinfolk . . . but never again did she take up a leadership role in the community.

As the third winter following Dag's forced departure from Alfheim slowly drew to a close, Aelas became increasingly restless. Having seen first-hand the fragility and uncertainty of life and love, her yearning for Dag's presence in her life grew almost unbearable. Throughout the spring and into the summer, the elf-maid and her dog were to be seen wandering, seemingly aimlessly, throughout the forests of Vuobmai . . . watching, waiting. Then came a day when a certain raven came to her and told of another wanderer and his dog who had just left Svartalfheim and were heading across the high fjell toward Vuobmai. Calling out her thanks to the bird, Aelas ran toward the most likely point of entry to the forest, no longer to wander— though still to wait. But not for long!

TWO HEARTS BEAT AS ONE

When I first saw Dag—with Ledgi padding along beside him—coming down off the high fjell toward the forested border of Vuobmai where Darra and I awaited them, I was assailed by an array of emotions. I knew that I loved him more deeply than ever . . . but how did he feel about me? I didn't question our connection as fang-mates, but Dag had never expressed a romantic interest in me before his exile, so why should I suppose that anything had changed? For all I knew, he could still be committed to his spirit-love, the giantess Brekka . . . or who knows what human girl might have captured his heart during the past three years. And, if she had, why not? We had had no special understanding when he left other than the hope I bore in the privacy of my heart.

Thus it was that our reunion was more subdued than I would have wished. True, we shared a prolonged hug, but there were no passionate kisses such as the one I had bestowed on Dag when he departed from Alfheim three long years ago. And when we started down the trail that would eventually bring us back to our village deep in the forest of Vuobmai, we walked hand-in-hand as might any long-separated brother and sister who cared for each other. Despite my strong feelings for Dag, I had resolved to wait until I could better determine where and how his feelings lay before I opened my heart on the subject. I was just too fearful of creating an awkward situation that might put our present relationship in jeopardy.

Early on, our walk was largely in silence, which permitted Dag to experience the simple pleasure of being back in Alfheim after such a long absence. As for me, I was content for the moment to enjoy the sight of him and feel the touch of his hand holding mine. After a time, we started to talk and soon were chattering on like two red squirrels about our respective adventures during our long separation. I was fascinated to hear about all of the places he had visited during his "out-wandering" as a storyteller, and he seemed to be equally intrigued to learn of my quests with Formindar.

"Oh, Aelas, how I wish I could have shared those adventures with you and my sworn-brother. To be able to save the life of a dragonet, then barely escape with your own from a fearsome Frost Giant . . . my dear girl, those deeds are the stuff of legends!"

"Well," I said, "you're welcome to add them to the collection of tales you tell. I only ask that you neither glorify nor make light of Hjaki's death. I had no choice in the matter if I didn't want him to crush Formindar . . . but to slay someone with your own hand and have to watch—and feel—him die, is a horrible experience to go through." I shuddered and added: "I don't know if I will ever get over it!"

Dag stopped and pulled me to him. "Aelas, Aelas, I am so sorry! I've seen loved ones die, but I never had to kill anyone. I can barely begin to imagine what that must have been like."

Describing the event had brought the memories flooding back and reopened the unhealed wound in my spirit. Tears came pouring out and I sobbed on Dag's chest as if my heart would break. Saying not a word, he just held me in his embrace until I had cried myself out. I heard Darra whining in sympathy and, looking down, beheld her and Dag's Ledgi regarding me with concern. Anxious to reassure her, I disengaged myself from my fang-mate's arms and, dropping to my knees, gave her a big hug. "You always know when I'm unhappy, don't you, sweetheart?"

After nuzzling Darra's neck for a few moments, I looked up at Dag and said: "Thank you for being so understanding. You must think I'm just an old cry-baby!"

"Not at all, Aelas. I, too, have felt such despair that it wrung out every tear I had in me to shed. Yet, when the flow had ebbed to a trickle, I saw my life's path in a new light . . . and that is why I am here with you now."

"Oh, my," I exclaimed. "Now that is a story I really must hear."

"And so you shall," Dag replied, "but it is a long one, so I hope you don't mind if we wait until we've had supper and settled down for the night."

I had been so caught up in the thrill of being together again—as well as by the stories we had already shared—I failed to notice that the sun was now low in the western sky. Furthermore, I also became aware that my stomach was complaining it was more than ready to be fed. Dag obviously was feeling the same way, so we focused our attention on finding a suitable campsite, one that was complete with good drinking water and a ground cover soft enough to permit comfortable sleeping.

Sure enough, with both of us scanning the land on either side of the trail, we soon came upon a babbling woodland brook, bordered on one side by a sloping mossy bank. It looked to be ideal for our purposes . . . and so it proved to be. Lacking fresh game to cook, we had no need for a fire, so we flopped down on the moss and opened our packs to see what kind of dried rations we could share with each other and our dogs. Darra and Ledgi were soon chewing contentedly on strips of deer meat, as were Dag and I—but we supplemented ours with chunks of good elvish moss bread.

We would have liked to wash the food down with a refreshing

mug of hot birch tea, but that pleasure would have to wait until we reached our village and had the means to boil water. Deprived of that creature comfort, we detached the birch burl cups we carried on our belts and Dag filled them for us from the sparkling stream that gurgled past our campsite. When we had drunk our fill of the clear, cold water, we sank back on the mossy bank and watched the sun disappear below the horizon, its glowing image partially interrupted by the silhouettes of the forest trees.

After a time, I hitched myself up on one elbow so I could face Dag, then asked him: "And now your story . . . ?"

"And now my story," he agreed. Dag then proceeded to tell me in great detail how he had entered Svartalfheim in search of the legendary Grotto of Grief. There he had hoped to learn the fate of his mother, the swan-maiden Hervor, only to discover that she was doomed to remain a swan for the rest of her days—a discovery that brought him great grief, indeed. It was bad enough that his beloved uncle and mentor, Ragnar Runewise, had been slain—as had his father, his half-brother, and his giantess sweetheart, Brekka. To add one more misery to all these others, Dag had been exiled from his Alfheim family with no assurance that he would ever see us again.

Small wonder that Dag was utterly overwhelmed by the loss of all his nearest kin and added his tears to the countless others that fill the grotto's mystical pool! On the brink of total despair and a complete emotional and spiritual collapse, he was called back to a sense of himself and a re-engagement with life through the sympathetic affection of his dog-companion, Ledgi. My own tears were running down my cheeks by this point in Dag's narrative.

"Oh, my dear fang-mate," I cried, "I am so sorry you had to experience all that pain. It must have been unbearable!"

"And unbearable it would have been save for Ledgi, bless his heart. Yet I did survive the trial and emerged the stronger for it. I was forced to look deep within my inner being, learn what was truly important to me, and—knowing that—decide what to do with the rest of my life."

"And what did you learn, Dag?" I asked quietly.

"I discovered that love is more important to me than anything else in the Nine Worlds . . . and that I can no longer bear to be separated from the ones I love. So here I am, my dear, and I don't want us to be parted ever again. If and when I take up Odin's storytelling charge once more, I will do so only if you are permitted to accompany me. You *would* like that, wouldn't you?" Dag asked anxiously.

"You know I would," I replied, "now more than ever. Those three years of out-wandering with Uncle Formindar really whetted my appetite for seeing different places and people. There is so much to learn about the Nine Worlds that can only come from first-hand experience . . . scary as that can be at times."

Dag breathed a deep sigh of relief. "I am so glad you feel that way. I was worried that you might never want to leave Alfheim again after your chilling encounter with Hjaki."

"There's no denying it was a terrible experience, but if I were to spend the rest of my life worrying about everything that *might* happen, I might just as well stay in my tent and never set foot outside it again . . . and that is no way for anyone to live. No, I'd prefer to take my chances and meet life as it comes."

"You are one of the bravest, most venturesome persons I know," Dag said admiringly. "That's one of the many things I love about you."

I did a double-take. Dag had never before used the word "love" with me in that tone of voice. Had his attitude toward me changed for the better since he'd been away? There was only one way to find out so, throwing caution to the winds, I took my heart in my hands and said: "Love, you just said, and it didn't sound to this elf-maid's sharp ears like you meant a simple brother-sister kind of affection. Are you talking about romantic love, or am I completely misunderstanding what's going on here?"

A sweet smile spread across Dag's open countenance. "No, Aelas dear, you didn't misunderstand a thing. One of the discoveries I made during my ordeal at the Grotto of Grief was that much as I missed my fang-mate, I wanted no, needed—you to be an even larger part of my life. Yes, my dearest, I now know that I love you deeply and passionately . . . and I want you to be my wife."

"Oh, Dag," I cried as I threw myself into his waiting arms. "I have waited for such a very long time to hear you say those words to me. I've loved you ever since our Great Hunt, but I never said anything because I didn't know how you felt."

"Then you *will* marry me?" He queried.

"I'd like nothing better," I responded, "but there is a problem."

"What in the Nine Worlds could that be?" Dag frowned. "You aren't committed to someone else, are you?"

"No," I replied, "but you are . . . or at least you were when last I saw you. I'm speaking of your long-dead sweetheart, Brekka, of course. I know her spirit continues to speak with you in your dreams, and if you are as deeply devoted to her now as you were then, how can you even speak to me of that kind of love? Doesn't it seem disloyal?"

There, my worst fear was out in the open . . . for good or for ill. What was I thinking, to risk pushing away my chance at happiness just when I was about to grasp it with both hands? But, much as I needed Dag, I knew I could not live a lie—pretending that Brekka didn't exist—nor would I let him do so either. You can't deny your feelings for long and, if Dag still loved Brekka, sooner or later she would come between us—as surely dead as if she still dwelt in the mortal realm.

"Believe me, Aelas, when I tell you that I understand your concerns—once, I shared them."

"You 'once' shared them? But not any longer?" I asked skeptically.

"No, not any longer—thanks to a conversation I had with Brekka a short time ago. Let me explain. When I first faced the reality of my feelings for you, I was racked with guilt. Brekka was my first love and we were inseparable up until the time of her death in the avalanche caused by Angrboda. I thought I had truly lost her forever, but through the good will of Freyja and Odin, she and I were permitted to reunite for a brief time in Asgard where our love even deepened. But no mortal man can remain long in the realm of the Gods, so the All-Father soon sent me off to Alfheim to further my education among my father's people—and you know the rest of that story, for you were a big part of it from the time Formindar brought me to your village until Odin sent me back to Midgard.

"I know I have told you that Odin made Brekka my *hamingja*— my guardian spirit—which has allowed her to visit me in my dreams when circumstances in my life required her help, whether to warn me of impending danger or to give me advice and encouragement. But, fortunately or unfortunately, my life has rarely been threatened, so many months go by without a visit from Brekka. I still love her—and always will—but the nature of our relationship has clearly changed and, as I have learned, no one was more aware of that than Brekka herself!"

"Why, what happened?" I asked him, my heart in my throat.

"As I said a moment ago, when I discovered the depth of my feelings for you, I did indeed feel that I was being disloyal to Brekka, just as you surmised. So it isn't surprising that when I tried to settle down to sleep that night, my mind was a battleground for my conflicted feelings . . . and I tossed and turned in despair. Finally, I must have drifted off to sleep somehow, for that is when it happened."

"When *what* happened?" I exclaimed.

"Brekka appeared to me, as clear and distinct to my eyes as you are now. 'Poor Dag,' she said, 'you are fretting yourself sick for no good reason. I am touched that you still love me as you do—and I love you as well—but believe me, dear man, when I tell you that I do not feel resentful of the love you bear for Aelas. You and I can no longer touch each other or spend much time together as the companions we once were. Ours is now a purely spiritual love, and that is something which is not finite in quantity but can be shared with others without diminishing anyone's portion. Our spiritual love shall never cease, but I want you to enjoy your mortal life with a loving partner to share your passions. And, should the two of you ever be blessed with a child or two, you can be sure I will be looking over them and guarding them as I have you. Fare thee well, my true love.'

"And with that, she faded from my sight and the dream ended. I was filled with a feeling of relief and joy—for the burden of guilt had been lifted, and I was free to declare my love for you. Brekka has given us her blessing, my dear, and I trust that will still your fears . . . and let you follow your heart. So, I ask once more, will you be my wife?"

"With all my heart, my dearest Dag! We can have Uncle Formindar conduct the wedding ritual as soon as we return to our village and announce our intentions. As for right now, let's seal our accord with a kiss." So kiss we did—passionately and more than once—and that night we slept in each other's arms.

The next day we hastened homeward for we were anxious to share our good news with my family and with the other villagers. But even before we reached the adjacent tents of Formindar and my parents—who by right and custom should be the first to be told of our betrothal—a wave of excitement swept through the village as other members of the community recognized Dag and welcomed him back. At first he just grinned and waved, but soon so many had gathered to greet him that we simply had to stop and let them do so . . . and to assure one and all that this time he was back to stay.

My parents and uncle had emerged from their tents by then to see what all of the hullabaloo was about, and when they beheld Dag—for the first time in three years—Formindar and my mother, Falan, rushed forward to embrace him. After all, Dag was my uncle's sworn-brother, while to my mother he had become like a son. Little did she realize he was soon to become her son by marriage. Skuttar, my father, was more restrained in his greeting, but when he clasped Dag's wrists and said gruffly: "It's good to have you back, boy," I could tell he really meant it.

At this point the other villagers dispersed to their own homes, leaving us some privacy to enjoy our family reunion. Falan sent Skuttar to one of the elevated storage sheds behind their tent to fetch enough meat and vegetables so that she could prepare a sumptuous evening meal for the five of us—not to mention bringing strips of dried meat for our dog-companions and Raiko. Formindar went with his brother-in-law to help retrieve the foodstuffs, which also included a loaf of moss-bread and a block of reindeer cheese. All that food, accompanied by mugs of honey-sweetened birch tea and wild berries, made for a real feast and we all ate our fill . . . and then some.

When the meal was over and we were reclining on the skin-covered birch-bough beds that partially encircled the central firepit, my family looked expectantly at Dag. Surely, they thought, he was about to relate the many adventures he had experienced during his exile—an anticipation voiced aloud by my mother.

"I will be only too happy to share those tales with you," he declared, "but first I want to talk to you about a great adventure that lies ahead . . . one that I have asked Aelas to share with me." He was speaking, of course, of our future life together as husband and wife, and he wasted no time in getting to that point. Anxious as we both were to receive their blessings on our union, Dag chose to forego his natural inclination as a storyteller to keep his audience in suspense as long as possible. When he concluded by asking my uncle to perform the wedding ritual for us as soon as elvish customs would deem it appropriate, my normally quiet family vigorously demonstrated their approval.

My mother hugged me tightly while declaring: "Oh, my darling girl, I am so happy for you. You could not have chosen a finer mate."

Meanwhile, Uncle Formindar clasped Dag's hands as he declared: "I had so hoped this joyful day would come—the betrothal of my beloved niece and my sworn-brother. Surely the Light has marked your paths. And yes, of course, I would be honored and delighted to conduct the ceremony to celebrate your union."

As for my father, Skuttar simply grinned and clapped Dag on the shoulder, saying only. "Welcome to the family, son."

My heart overflowed with joy as my family's acceptance and love surrounded and embraced Dag and me. Here, truly, was our home, and so it would remain no matter where in the Nine Worlds Dag's storytelling might lead us. What the future held in store for us was, of course, unclear—as it is for every being—but we knew we could face it with hope and courage, for we would be doing so together!

Epilogue

The traditional ceremony that ritually united Aelas Falansdottir and Dag Völundsson took place at dawn three days later in the presence of the entire village. Standing on the west side of a flickering fire formed by four small birch logs arranged in the shape of *gebo*, the love rune, the couple exchanged rings woven from very narrow strips of birchbark. Intoning the traditional declaration: "Let our two hearts now beat as one," they responded to Formindar's ritual command "Enter you now into the Light" by holding hands and leaping in unison high over the fire. As they landed—unscathed—the first rays of the rising sun illuminated their faces, and Formindar cried out: "They have entered into the Light, indeed. Now, truly their two hearts beat as one!"

With that declaration, the ceremony was concluded, but the wedded life of Aelas and Dag had just begun.

AFTERWORD:

LURE AND LORE OF THE LIGHT ELVES

Much as I love the Norse myths and legends as a whole, I have always been particularly intrigued by those that feature elves or dragons—or better yet, both—which may explain why they turn up in so many of my own stories. I don't pretend to fully understand either group and, in fact, one of the reasons I write these tales is to try to learn more about them.

If you are thinking that what I have just written sounds a bit strange, I must confess I thought so as well the first time I read something similar in another author's book. Then I began to write my Nine Worlds stories and soon discovered that the act of writing fiction seems to open a doorway into the Unconscious, wherein dwell our imagination and our dreams—both of which appear to have lives of their own. While we can consciously guide the former—much of the time—strange twists and turns of plot and characters often emerge unexpectedly. And it is a wise author who heeds this voice of the Unconscious and does not attempt to suppress it in favor of a pre-planned, rigidly structured formula. While a skilled writer might be able to ignore the voice and still produce something readable, such a story would not be nearly so much fun to write . . . and its author would have to forego an opportunity to learn more about his/her own Unconscious.

The elves in this book are intended to be the Light Elves of Norse mythology, as distinct from the Norse Dark Elves (generally thought to be another name for the Dwarves), the Celtic Sidhe (who were thought to live in an underworld setting accessible to humans only through temporary openings in mounds), and the wee, often winged Fairies of Victorian England. There are several references in the Icelandic Eddas that point to the Saami people (formerly called Lapps) as the inspiration for the concept of Light Elves in the minds of Viking-Age Scandinavians, and it is for this reason that I have drawn largely upon traditional Saami society in characterizing the material culture and lifestyles of the Light Elves. My principal sources for this information have included (but not been limited to) *Turi's Book of Lapland* by Johan Turi, *The Lapps* by Björn Collinder, *The Lapps* by Roberto Bosi, *People of Eight Seasons* by Ernst Manker, and various articles in *Baiki* magazine. But the reader should be warned—my Light Elves are *not* identical to the Saami, and where the culture of the latter lacked some device or behavior I deemed necessary to further the plot or add atmosphere, I had no qualms about turning to my imagination to supply what was needed.

All elvish words were taken directly from the Saami language or, in some instances, have been modified for easier pronunciation by English speakers. Each personal and place-name was carefully chosen so that its Saami meaning would accurately reflect some aspect of that person or place. A pronunciation guide appears on pages 98-100.

The lucky crow's feather mentioned in "Heart of the Sun, Heart of a Dragon" actually was a traditional Saami folk-belief, and the "thunderstone"—which appears in "Heart of a Dwarf" and plays such a decisive role in "Heart of Ice"—was described in the Icelandic tale called *Thorstein's Saga*. And that most intriguing and fearsome of birds—the Gammer—played an important part in the Icelandic *Saga of Arrow-Odd*.

Finally, I should mention something about the Light, of which Formindar speaks rather frequently. To my imperfect understanding of the matter, the Light is an impersonal, but positive spiritual force that sometimes seems to subtly shape events in the Nine Worlds . . . possibly behaving in a manner similar to that of the Viking-Age concept called *wyrd*. Perhaps *wyrd* is one manifestation of the Light! In any event, the Light is not a capricious god-form such as Odin, nor is it equivalent to "the Force" of *Star Wars* fame, for the Light is not subject to manipulation for good or ill like "the Force." One can only strive to bring one's life into alignment with the Light . . . the attainment of which brings its own reward. And that, of course, is the goal of the Alfar Way discussed at some length in *The Dragonseeker Saga*.

PRONUNCIATION GUIDE FOR ELVISH NAMES

The following is a guide to the pronunciation and literal meaning of proper names appearing in Alflagan, the language of the Light Elves, in my three Nine Worlds books—*Theft of the Sun* (TS), *The Dragonseeker Saga* (DS), and *Way of the Elves* (WE). The first appearance of the character or place is indicated by two initials. For each name, the stressed syllable is capitalized. Where the sound "eh" appears, it should be pronounced like the "a" in "fate." A word of warning: although Alflagan largely follows the Saami language, any similarity in pronunciation is purely coincidental!

Finally, because he is a major character, I should mention that Dag has a Norwegian—not an Elvish—name . . . and it should be pronounced *DAHG.*

Aelas (DS)—*EH-lahs*: lively, spirited

Aika (DS)—*EYE-kah*: a great big tree

Aratak (TS)—*AHR-ah-tak*: one whom nothing can stop

Arke (DS)—*AHR-keh*: miserable, sad

Arvel (TS)—*AHR-vehl*: brave, undaunted

Bissovas (WE)—*bee-SOH-vahs*: one who is steadfast

Boatka (WE)—*boh-AHT-kah*: a narrow strip between two lakes; a mountain pass

Darra (DS)—*DAHR-ah*: having a greatly curved tail

Darse (WE)—*DAHR-seh*: a short, fat male

Dattulas (WE)—*DAHT-yoo-lahs*: one who is willing

Duodda (DS)—*doo-OH-dah*: a high mountain moorland

Duostel (WE)—*doo-OHS-tel*: daring, bold, intrepid

Eren (TS)—*EHR-en*: one who keeps separate from others

Falan (DS)—*FAH-lahn*: one who is quick and ready

Fawro (TS)—*FAW-roh*: lovely, beautiful

Formindar (DS)—*FOHR-min-dahr*: the guardian

Girkad (TS)—*GEER-kahd*: bright-eyed; he of the piercing eye

Haewdne (DS)—*HAH-ood-neh*: an orb-weaving spider

Haksel (TS)—*HAHK-sel*: one who has an acute sense of smell

Hillai (TS)—*hill-EYE*: full of glowing, live embers

Jallo (WE)—*YAH-loh*: daring, bold, fearless

Laeksa (DS)—*LEHK-sah*: a large valley, often containing a
    spring or river source

Lawlo (DS)—*LAW-loh*: one who sings

Ledgi (TS)—*LEHD-gee*: grayish brown and quick as lightning

Linu (DS)—*LEE-noo*: having a sleek grey, or nearly black, coat

Manne (DS)—*MAH-neh*: one who goes very far; far-roving

Maras (DS)—*MAHR-ahs*: a large hill, covered with birches,
    usually surrounded by bogs and small lakes

Merin (DS)—*MEH-rin*: seacoast dwellers

Muöre (WE)—*MEW-reh*: an authoritative, masterful woman

Muorra (DS)—*moo-OH-rah*: full of trees

Njalmadak (WE)—*NYAHL-mah-dahk*: part of a fjord near
    its mouth

Njuolgalas (TS)—*nyoo-OHL-gah-las*: sensible, dependable, honest

Njalla (DS)—*NYAH-lah*: ice fox

Njuollo (TS)—*nyoo-OH-loh*: arrow; nickname for one who is
    very quick

Oaivalas (TS)—*oh-EYE-vah-lahs*: one who is clever, intelligent

Oavar (TS)—*OH-ah-vahr*: bold, daring

Raiko (WE)—*RYE-koh*: a wild young rascal

Rehalas (WE)—*reh-HAH-lahs*: upright, honorable, honest

Riddo (TS)—*REE-doh*: beach, seashore

Sietha (DS)—*see-EH-thah*: dawn

Siskebu (WE)—*SIS-keh-boo*: that which is farther in

Skaldo (DS)—*SKAHL-doh*: a big, fine-looking man

Skuttar (WE)—*SKOO-tahr*: one who shoots well

Stadok (TS)—*STAHD-ohk*: one who is very steady and trustworthy

Stuoravuodna (WE)—*STOO-oh-rah:voo-OHD-nah*: big fjord

Suonjar (WE)—*soo-OHN-yahr*: a beam of light

Tsiwakan (WE)—*tsee-WAH-kahn*: a woman who talks in a
  low voice

Urka (WE)—*OOR-kah*: a person of exceptionally small size

Valdai (TS)—*VAHL-dye*: domineering, possessive, self-willed

Varrai (WE)—*vah-RYE*: having many mountains

Varvis (TS)—*VAHR-vis*: possessing sharp sight or quick hearing

Vassai (WE)—*VAHS-eye*: spiteful, ill-natured

Vavsun (TS)—*VAHV-soon*: one who watches

Verdi (WE)—*VEHR-dee*: a guest-friend

Vuobmai (WE)—*voo-OHB-my*: where there is a lot of woodland

PRINCIPLES OF
THE ALFAR WAY

These principles that characterize the world-view of the Light Elves are described and elaborated upon on pages 89-94 of *The Dragonseeker Saga*.

YGGDRASIL
THE WORLD TREE, UNITING THE NINE WORLDS

This bonus story represents the first chapter in the next Nine Worlds Saga, **The Walker in Shadows***. The tale is set in Midgard during the period of Dag's exile from Alfheim, and it introduces a unique and mysterious new protagonist, Faragrim, the Walker in Shadows.*

TROLLS IN THE MIST

Gudmund paused, panting, beside a moss-covered boulder that partially leaned over the trail up which he had been hastening for what seemed like an eternity. When he left his sod-roofed cabin in the valley that morning, the sky had been clear with just a hint of fall in the crisp air—a perfect day to make the trek up and over the rugged ridge of the Troll's Teeth to pay a long-delayed visit to his brother Arne in Kverndal.

All had gone well until he stopped to eat the bread and cheese he had in his backpack. Knowing that he was more than half way to his destination, Gudmund decided he could afford to stretch out on a mossy bank and catch a quick nap. After all, his stomach was full and the sun was warm . . . what could possibly be the harm in it?

A man who had survived in this region to become Gudmund's age—nearly forty—should have known better. The mountains are beautiful, 'tis true enough, but they are also as changeable as a young maid's fancies. Gudmund realized this the moment a sudden drop in the temperature woke him from a deep slumber and pleasant dreams. The sun was nowhere to be seen, and not only were dark, lowering clouds filling the sky, but a dense mist had begun to spread along the ridge crest and flow down toward the valleys below.

Clearly it was high time for Gudmund to be on his way if he hoped to reach Kverndal before sunset. Moreover, these mountains were no place to be after dark, for many a troll called them home . . . and those fierce creatures loved nothing more than a taste of human flesh! Gudmund started off at a brisk pace, muttering under his breath at his own carelessness, and praying that the mist wouldn't thicken so much that he couldn't see the trail. He had traveled this way often enough to know that countless side paths branched off hither and thither, so he needed to be able to see familiar landmarks lest he stray off the right path.

Alas for Gudmund, the mist thickened to the point that all he could see of the trail was the part just a few feet in front of him. He was strongly tempted to hunker down right where he was to spend the night—cold and uncomfortable as that would be—and wait for the morning sun to disperse the mist. But then he heard a sound that chilled his blood and sent him scrambling blindly along what he hoped was still the right trail—it was the deep, hooting cries of trolls a'hunting!

Ordinarily, trolls venture out only at night for they are petrified of being struck by the sun's rays, which are said to turn trolls to stone. But on days such as this, when the sun's rays are blocked by mist or rain, some of the more daring trolls are emboldened to risk wandering out and about. Such were the ones that apparently had caught scent of Gudmund and were now on his trail—or so he surmised, for their hoots surely seemed to be drawing closer.

There, looming out of the mist on the trail just behind him, that huge dark shape could only be a troll! Panic seized Gudmund and he lurched ahead with no thought in his head now save to outrun and escape his pursuers. Soon he came to a fork in the trail and, without hesitation, darted up the right-hand path, praying as he did that his sinister followers would choose to take the other one—forgetting for the moment that the long-nosed trolls have a keen sense of smell!

The path ascended sharply, then seemed to level out—though where it was headed, Gudmund neither saw nor cared. Suddenly, a powerful hand reached out and grasped his arm in an iron grip while a soft, rasping voice whispered in his ear: "Not another step would I take on this path, my friend, unless you're Hel-bound to spend this night in the icy embrace of Loki's daughter. The cliff face is broken off here, and the next solid ground lies three hundred feet below. Come aside, come aside."

Gudmund stammered his thanks to his rescuer, whom he could not clearly see because of the dense mist and the fact that the man's face—if a man he was—was hidden by a deep hood. But even at that, Gudmund could almost have sworn that he saw two gleaming points of light deep within the hood where the man's eyes should be. How could that be possible, thought Gudmund, I must be imagining things.

Any further speculation was cut short by a hissed exclamation from his companion: "It seems we have company. Here come three trolls. Hide yourself beneath the low overhang on the right, and don't move no matter what happens. I'll deal with these trolls. Quickly now!"

"He can't have gone far," snarled the leading troll, "the man odor is ripe in me nose. We'll have him soon."

"That's quite far enough, Kraki," rasped the hooded figure. "The man you seek is under my protection now." So saying, he stepped fully into the trail and held up his staff forbiddingly. Its splayed, three-pronged head—carved and polished from a piece of moose antler—was suggestive of *algiz*, the rune of protection.

"Curse you for meddling again, Faragrim . . . or whatever your real name is," growled the troll. "Me and the boys picked up his trail first, so he's our meat. Just because you call yourself the 'Walker in Shadows' don't give you no right to spoil our hunt."

"You know that I have every right to do so! These mountains are my home now, and I've told you before that I will not tolerate having my human neighbors harrassed or killed by trolls—or anyone else. Heed my warnings and you'll have no trouble from me. Continue to ignore them and I'll make you wish you'd never been born."

"Think yer somethin', don't you?" snarled Kraki. "Well, we're not afraid of you or your silly-looking rune staff. We're bigger than you and stronger than you, and there are three of us. So the way I figger it, when we get through with you there won't be enough of you left to feed a rat. Get him, boys!"

Kraki stepped back to let his two followers lead the charge. Faragrim ducked aside from the rush of the first troll, and thrust his staff between the troll's feet as he ran past. This caused the troll to lose his balance and stumble so badly that his momentum carried him—arms flailing wildly—over the edge of the cliff and onto the rocks far below.

Not pausing to see what had happened behind him, Faragrim met the second troll with a hard thrust to the gut with the blunt antler butt of his staff, the blow buckling the troll over. Before the troll could recover his breath, Faragrim struck him on the side of the head with a sweeping blow that brought the troll crashing to his knees. Then, reversing his staff, Faragrim jammed the three-pronged head into the troll's left armpit and shoved so hard that this troll also toppled over the cliff, wailing as he fell.

When Kraki saw how easily Faragrim had disposed of his two henchmen, the troll suddenly decided he had urgent business elsewhere.

"It seems there is more than one reason to fear a rune staff, eh, Kraki? Heh, heh, heh, heh, heh, heh, heh!" This raspy, chuckling taunt, eerily echoing through the mist, followed the troll down the trail and haunted his dreams for a long time thereafter.

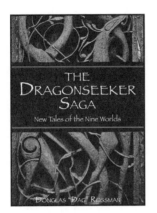

THE
DRAGONSEEKER
SAGA
New Tales of the Nine Worlds

DOUGLAS "DAG" ROSSMAN

The Dragonseeker Saga
New Tales of the Nine Worlds
Paperback, 144 pages, ISBN 978-1-57534-077-7

"*The Dragonseeker Saga* . . . is simultaneously a collection of nine stories and a short novella focused on one character: Dag Ormseeker. That structure brings the best features of both oral and written stories together. Read as tales, each story is a chapter in the book; but read as a book, or full narrative, each chapter is its own story where one remains captivated by the events at hand yet gradually builds up a larger context, story upon story, that leaves one with a richer sense of meaning from the saga of Dag Ormseeker.

'The Final Lesson' holds the single-most compelling image in the book—something utterly Norse in character and outlook, yet modern at the same time. I won't ruin the reading of it for you by telling you what it is, but look for a different take on the Well.

Ultimately, Dag's stories, like all true tales, speak to that which is timeless. In this collection, the truths told are about love and grief, how each is inseparable from the other and often more meaningful by that intertwined relationship. In Dag's tales, wyrd is not so much fate or the weight of the past or the consequences of our actions. Rather, wyrd is how we live our lives both in the comfort of the bonds of love and kinship and through the loss of that comfort when those we love die. To follow one's wyrd is to follow one's heart, honoring the bonds we share with those we love and for whom we grieve when they have left this life."

- reviewed by Dan Campbell
Idunna: A Journal of Northern Tradition

Theft of the Sun
and Other New Norse Myths
Paperback, 142 pages, ISBN 1-57534-015-1

"Douglas Rossman's Norse tales have appeared in *The Mythic Circle* from time to time; they are well-written, managing to find a balance point between the sometimes obscure or difficult to comprehend translations of the old tales and updatings that seem to place contemporary characters in the Norse costumes, dragging with them all the angst and anti-sense of wonder of modern times. Rossman keeps the Norse flavor while adding depth and interest to the characters, a difficult feat. . . .

The stories are vividly written, Norse in feel, rich in magic, humor, weird beasts, dwarves, and poems. . . . Rossman's stories vary in tone and length, exhibiting his expertise with the material, his style and engaging blend of the old and the new. The tales would read aloud well; I can imagine a group of children sitting round a hearth listening with 'bated breath to these stories, and then wishing to find out more about the mysteries of the ancient northern world."

- reviewed by Sherwood Smith
Mythprint

"Douglas 'Dag' Rossman is an American storyteller of Norse descent who put together *Theft of the Sun and Other New Norse Myths*. Rossman weaves the spell of the oral tradition behind his retelling of the old tales; his works are thus best read aloud. He also has written some original stories to account for what he considers loose ends in the classic tales, that is, he fills in the places where he wondered 'what happened next...?' I wholeheartedly agree with Jodie Forrest when in her introduction she compares Rossman with Hans Christian Andersen, I wish Mr. Rossman a long and productive writing career."

- *Green Man Review*
www.greenmanreview.com

The Nine Worlds:
A Dictionary of Norse Mythology

Paperback, 112 pages, ISBN 1-57534-014-3

"In *The Nine Worlds: A Dictionary of Norse Mythology*, author Douglas 'Dag' Rossman provides readers with an annotated list of the principal mythological beings, places, and magical implements mentioned in the Eddas — tales of Viking Age Scandinavia. But *The Nine Worlds* is more than a handy reference book, for its thoughtful preface places Norse mythology in a context we can understand today. In it, Rossman explains, in fascinating detail, the Viking-age belief system. . . .

Known for his passionate retellings of Norse myths and Viking tales, 'Dag' Rossman is a gifted storyteller who shares a passion for Norse mythology with his wife Sharon, an artist. A dozen of Sharon Rossman's detailed pen-and-ink illustrations illuminate the text of *The Nine Worlds*."

- Viking Heritage Magazine

These titles are available from:

Skandisk, Inc.

Tel. 952-829-8998 • 800-468-2424 • www.skandisk.com

DOUGLAS "DAG" ROSSMAN

Douglas "Dag" Rossman is the author of six books on the subject of Norse mythology. His original stories, most of them set in the Nine Worlds of Norse mythology, have appeared in the Sons of Norway's *Viking* magazine and *Mythic Circle* magazine. His storytelling skills are in great demand at folk festivals, heritage camps, and other Scandinavian events.

A biology professor at Louisiana State University for more than 35 years, "Dag" and his wife Sharon now live in Decorah, Iowa. Together, they created a major exhibit at the Vesterheim Norwegian-American Museum entitied *Echoes of Odin: Norse Mythology in Scandinavia and America*, and served as consultants for the Smithsonian traveling exhibition—*Vikings: The North Atlantic Saga* at the Minnesota Science Museum.